The
Good Husband's
Guide to
Balancing Hobbies
& Marriage

Steve
Chapman

HARVEST HOUSE PUBLISHERS

EUGENE, OREGON

Cover by Koechel Peterson & Associates, Inc., Minneapolis, Minnesota

THE GOOD HUSBAND'S GUIDE TO BALANCING HOBBIES AND MARRIAGE
Copyright © 2005 by Steve Chapman
Published by Harvest House Publishers
Eugene, Oregon 97402
www.harvesthousepublishers.com

Library of Congress Cataloging-in-Publication Data

Chapman, Steve.
    The good husband's guide to balancing hobbies and marriage / Steve Chapman
      p. cm.
    ISBN-13: 978-0-7369-1663-9 (pbk.)
    ISBN-10: 0-7369-1663-6 (pbk.)
    1. Husbands—Religious life. 2. Hobbies—Religious aspects—Christianity. I. Title.
    BV4528.3.C43 2005
    248.8'425—dc22   2005001510

Printed in the United States of America

    05 06 07 08 09 10 11 12 / BP-MS / 10 9 8 7 6 5 4 3 2 1

Dedication and Thanks

*This writing is dedicated to the one person
who most deserves my thanks for inspiring this book.
She is my dear wife, Annie.*

*A special thanks is also extended to the
husbands and wives who shared their valuable time
and completed the questionnaires that were used
as a part of this text. You know who you are, and
your vulnerability was a gift for which I
will be forever grateful.*

Contents

A Note from the Author

This book is about husbands and wives and how the marital relationship can be affected by what the man likes to do recreationally. The words *hobby*, *interest*, *habit*, *obsession*, and *passion* can be used interchangeably throughout the text to identify the activities that husbands enjoy.

This book offers ideas and guidelines that are intended to strengthen the quality of your marriage. The pages are filled with the insights and thoughts of one husband (an avid hunter) who has learned how to live in harmony with his wife for more than three decades. They will help you find the right balance between your marriage and hobby.

—Steve Chapman

Introduction

Back in the late 1990s, I wrote a book based on my passion for hunting. It's entitled *A Look at Life from a Deer Stand.* Amazingly, more than 200,000 readers have picked it up since its release. And add to that an unknown number of folks who may have consumed a copy placed on coffee tables at deer camps and lodges across our nation. To say the very least, I am delighted that so many folks have enjoyed the writing. Thankfully, I have a file cabinet full of letters that contain heartwarming comments from those who share my joy of the "fair chase."

Although hunting is my first love when it comes to hobbies, I also dabble in a few others. I enjoy hiking, bicycling, and motorcycling. I fish, kayak, and camp. I own basketballs, baseball gloves, and golf clubs. And that doesn't count the sports—such as auto racing—that I watch in person and on TV. If I let it, sports could occupy my every waking moment...and I would be perfectly happy and content. Okay, not really...but close.

Life—at least my life...and probably yours—isn't made up of just sports. We have to balance our passion for hobbies with the love and responsibilities of the truly major things in life, such as our wives, our families, our occupations, our spiritual lives and related commitments, our community endeavors, and our other less-important but essential activities. In this book, we're going to focus on one of the most primary relationships we have...our loving partnership with our wives.

Since the release of *A Look at Life from a Deer Stand*, I have had many opportunities to hear from ladies who are married to hunters. As a result, I have discovered that conflicting feelings exist between husbands and mates when it comes to pursuing hobbies. While many of the wives said that by reading my book they got a clearer picture of why their husbands loved to hunt, they still had unsettling issues they dealt with in regard to their husbands' passions. Concerns such as budget strains on the family economy, communication divides, and the emotional stress related to worrying about the inherent dangers involved in hunting are just a few that unhappy wives have voiced.

But hobbies don't have to have a negative impact on marriage. It is my hope that this book will help the "obsessed" husband regain the favor of his wearied, worried wife. That goal alone was plenty of motivation, but one other thing drove me to continue writing. I know at least one wife who does not hate her husband's love for his hobby. That woman is my bride, Annie. While it has not been easy to maintain her favor for what I love to do, the peace and joy that such an accomplishment contributes to our marriage—and the ways I have managed to do it—are things I desperately long to pass on to other men. I want you to know the joy of a contented wife too!

Keep in mind that because my primary passion is hunting, the tips I offer in these pages are illustrated with stories from that activity. However, the efforts I have made toward *not* alienating my bride will help husbands with all types of hobbies. My main qualification for writing this book is that I am a sportsman with a happy wife…a contented wife…a wife who supports my hobbies. And, by the way, if you don't think it is important to do all that you can to cultivate the sweet disposition of contentment in your wife, consider this ancient bit of wisdom from the book of Proverbs (27:15):

> A constant dripping on a day of steady rain and a contentious woman are alike….

Applying that ancient text to the subject of this book suggests that unless you really enjoy constant confrontations about your hobby, you would do well to do all you can do to keep the sun shining on your marital relationship.

If you are not a fan of the hunt, yet this subject has captured your attention, there is hope for you too. Included in this writing are not just some of my stories, but also the thoughts of many other sportsmen such as golfers, fishermen, skiers, campers, hikers, photographers, and motorcyclists to name a few. These men, as well as their wives, have anonymously contributed to the text by completing a nonscientific survey. These questionnaires contained some very probing inquiries about the effects that a man's hobbies can have on his marriage. Their input yields a necessary and very important balance to this book. The truth is, not every husband hunts, but so many of us who have hobbies have at least one thing in common—a tendency to overdo the doing!

I believe Annie has said it best: "Very simply, if a wife hates what her husband loves to do, then he's not doing it right!"

Gentlemen, if the title of this book caught your eye and made you cringe a bit, then you should take the time to read it. Admittedly, there are some challenges in this text that might represent some mountains for you to climb. Do you care enough about your marriage to make the ascent? *Yes?* Then read on. Or men, if your wives bought this book for you, go ahead and give these time-tested tips a try. Every little bit helps when it comes to marriage.

1

A Quick Fix

It was a day in late July when I returned home from a trip to our local archery shop. I exited the truck, and on my way into the house I walked by my wife, Annie, who was working in her garden. When she looked up to greet me, the brightly colored feathers on the freshly made dozen arrows I caressed caught her keen eyes. Nodding and looking toward the tight bundle of camo-painted aluminum shafts, Annie recognized what they were and spoke with a sweet-yet-concerned tone in her voice.

"Did you need another dozen arrows?"

Suddenly the air was silent. I knew three things in that moment. I knew very well that she was aware of the big bucket in our garage that held the huge number of arrows I had already collected. And I assumed that in her estimation the arrows that were in that bucket probably seemed in perfectly good condition. Second, she was also very much aware that a goodly amount of cash was probably paid for the new dozen. Thus, the understandable motivation behind her question. And third, I knew I had better come up with an answer that made perfect economic sense.

I could have attempted an explanation, for example, that my purchase was a matter of personal safety due to the violent actions generated by the opposing forces inherent in the operational mechanics of the collapsing limbs on a compound bow during a shot. For that reason, the arrow shaft leaving the shelf rest of the bow must be in the best of condition for unfailing performance. The great comfort it would be for her to know that my new, strong, unused, dependable arrows could ultimately contribute to her husband's safe and unharmed return from the woods would have been a good thing to mention.

Or I could have told her how merciful and humane a well-made shot with a perfectly tuned arrow can be to the deer, and that excellent arrow placement has much to do with the archer's confidence in his equipment.

I could have said these intelligent things. But no. In a voice that bore a striking resemblance to that of Ernest T. Bass, I blurted out, "Oh yeah, Baby, a feller's gotta have new straight sticks every year."

Sadly, my words lacked eloquence and grace, as well as the slightest sign of good sense. Thankfully, Annie didn't say anything. She just shook her head and went on about her summer-day chore of watering her garden. I went quietly into the house and nursed the sting of what had just happened. The barb of realizing that she harbored a question about my expenditure was painful. However, I did what too many of us guys do when we know our wives are not totally happy about something: I forgot about it. Many weeks later I had to face the fact that Annie had not forgotten.

In mid-October, when we had just finished dining at a local restaurant, the sobering truth about her feelings was revealed. The restaurant was one of those establishments that has a craft shop adjacent to the dining area. I paid the tab and was slipping the receipt into my pocket when I turned around and saw Annie across the room standing at a spinning rack of Christmas ornaments. Hanging off her pretty little hard-working fingers dangled three or four of the sparkling items. I immediately realized that she was planning a purchase. Knowing the extent of the decorations that already filled our attic, I stepped to her side and asked, "What are you doing?"

I'd like to let you believe that my question was delivered with a soft, sweet, understanding tone—the kind that makes a husband sound charming and attractive. However, if words had knives, Annie would have had to have stitches. My voice was elevated, yet subdued enough not to draw a crowd. Translated, I was really saying, "We have enough ornaments already!" However, Annie took my original question at face value and gave an answer that I will never forget. In response to my, "W*hat are you doing*?" she said... "I'm buying arrows!"

The blood ran to my feet as the verbal dart I had just thrown bounced off of her answer. Furthermore, there was a chilling air of confidence in her voice that informed me that I would have no problem remembering why she was responding the way she did. I was defenseless.

What did I do? I did what any smart man would do in a moment when he has been stripped of his armor down to his boxers. I went to the truck and waited quietly for her to complete her purchase and join me for the journey home.

"I'm buying arrows" has become my mental reminder through the years that I must show some fairness when it comes to money. Hardly an expenditure goes by that I don't recall seeing her beautiful-but-piercing green eyes as she turned and spoke to me that day in the restaurant. I honestly admired the bravery that it took for her to let me know she had not forgotten about my arrows.

To this day, I continue to appreciate the sense of fairness that her courageous response led me to find.

I can tell you without reservation that of the things I strive to do in order to help Annie not resent my love for my "hobby," my willingness to be fair when it comes to our money that I spend is probably the most noticeable. It may not be at the very top of the list in terms of importance, as you'll see later in the book, but it can definitely be an immediately tangible and hopeful sign to a woman that her husband cares about what she thinks. It is from my own personal success that I offer this first helpful tip. Though it could be classified as a "quick fix," in no way is it temporary. The benefits of it will last a lifetime.

The Equal Cash Method

After our "arrow/ornament" conflict had passed, and I had some time to think about the experience, an idea came to me that has yielded fantastic results. The good news is that it is so simple even the most dense of husbands can do it. (And that includes me!) I relay this idea to you with full confidence that your life as a husband-with-a-hobby will be revolutionized.

Here's how the idea works for me: Let's say that I'm in that big store where hunters and fishermen go to drool over the mountain of goodies on the endless shelves. There I see an item I have to have. For example, the item is a mechanical release for my bow string. I'm now looking at the price tag and it reads "$44.99." Prior to the arrow/ornament experience, I would have tossed it in the shopping cart, wiped the slurpy juices from my mouth, and headed to the next aisle. Not this time. As I'm deciding if it is the one that will bring me total

The Good Husband's Principle

Practice "price-tag doubling"

happiness as an archer, I suddenly hear the echo of, "I'm buying arrows." At that moment I'm reminded to do what I call Price-Tag Doubling.

Very simply, the numbers on the sticker pasted to the release is no longer $44.99. Now it reads $89.98. Why did the price double? Because I don't want my wife to hate what I love to do! In order to accomplish this goal, I know that things must be equal between Annie and me when it comes to spending money. Therefore, I quietly say to myself, "If I get this release, I'll need to go to my wallet or to the bank and take out $45 in cash and give it to Annie when I get home."

Whenever I have done this, more times than not, she has been so grateful for the fair treatment that she doesn't even ask what I bought! That is always a nice by-product. The truth is that if I can't be fair to her in this way for whatever reason (lack of funds, for example), then I know I should not purchase the item.

As I debate with myself in the store, I make a conscious choice either for my marriage or against it. To consider my purchase as any less in importance is to literally weaken my relationship with my wife. If I refuse to consider how she will feel about my investment, as small as it may be, then I will have knowingly put myself first in the matter. And herein lies the greatest danger for any husband who wants to enjoy his hobby free of guilt. When we constantly put our own interests above that of our wives', we risk sowing the seeds of contempt in her heart for the thing we love to do. If we sow enough of those ill seeds and consistently water them with an unequal usage of money, we will reap the sad harvest of our wives' resentment.

One important note about the "price-tag doubling" method. Keep in mind that I am not suggesting that it be applied to each and every purchase you make. It works best with items that cost anywhere from a few dollars to perhaps a couple of hundred, depending on your budget capabilities. In no way do I suggest that large items such as fishing boats, motorcycles, airplanes, or any other items of that size and significance be considered as a candidate for this method. Purchasing expensive "toys" such as these should *always* be talked over and mutually agreed upon.

Since I enacted this method several years ago, it has accomplished two important things in my life as a husband. First, the mental calculations involved with "price-tag doubling" has done wonders in regard to my exercising spend control. I'm a much more careful shopper. Issues such as product quality and finding the best prices have become much more important to me. The second very positive outcome from this method has been that being fair with my wife has won me some real points in the "being the best hubby" contest. And, as any deer hunter knows, "points" are important!

What Women Are Saying

For any husband who may be reading this and thinking you'd like to jack my jaw for even suggesting the idea of "price-tag doubling," please take a look at the following statements from wives as it pertains to their men, money, and fairness. Their comments are taken from a huge bundle of questionnaires that I collected from outdoorsmen and their wives over a two-year period. The long list of questions they answered included an inquiry about spending. For the wives the question was: *If you could say one thing to him about money spent for his hobby/interest, what would you say?* I have added some commentary on some of their responses.

❑ *I'd like to have money to spend on my desires too, but there are more important needs right now—like our kids.* (Wife of a husband who hunts)

❏ *Where is the balance? Between our regular monthly expenditures, unexpected things the kids need, and the other usual costs of keeping a family afloat, why does your hobby always have to take the most out of our budget?* (Wife of a husband who hunts *and* fishes)

❏ *The stuff you buy is way too expensive. If you're not competing and winning money while riding, why the need for a [bicycle] frame made of titanium, carbon fiber, etc.? And surely the clothes don't have to match the frame!* (Wife of a bicycling husband)

Obviously this wife considers the expense involved in her mate's passion for the sport of cycling excessive. There are two opposing dynamics at work in this marriage. If she refuses to appreciate what he loves to do, she runs the risk of pushing him away emotionally. If he fails to appreciate her concern for the funds he outlays for his equipment (his bike cost $3500), he jeopardizes the respect he longs to receive from her. I have to wonder if the bicycle purchase was mutually agreed upon. This couple provides a clear lesson about the value of fairness in the area of money and hobbies.

❏ *Think before you spend!* (Wife of a deer hunter)

The words in this statement are the type that can come at a man like a set of bear claws. In case you're asking, "Think about what?" let me give you some help. She wants him to think about: a) Does he *need* it? b) Can *we* afford it? c) Can he *get through the season without it?* On and on the implications of her short sentence go. Admittedly, men are notorious for being unable to read the lines between their wives' words! A smart husband would hear her statement this way:

> *Think* (She apparently has some feelings about the cost of
> this item. I wonder what they are?)...*before* (I *must* always

ask myself this question prior to writing the check and make sure I get an answer.)...*you* (I have a feeling that the word *you* means *me,* and that she thinks *me* has failed in times past with being smart with money. Have I?)...*spend* (an action that requires parting with funds that might be needed in another area of family life other than my hobby).

❑ *When the price tag is on the higher side, could we talk about it first or at least let me know that you bought something? It's not so nice to find out later from someone else!* (Her husband flies airplanes and operates a ham radio)

Yikes! I detect a crash landing about to happen with this ace if he continues on this course.

❑ *I wish you wouldn't be so impulsive!* (Wife of an avid hiker)

Once again, much is said with just a few words. Though I don't know this couple personally, I know about hiking and the expense involved with obtaining top-notch equipment. It's amazing how much "lightweight" can cost. You'd think that the heavier the gear, the more dollars it would require to get it. This is not so in the world of the hiker/camper. Amazingly, we can walk into an outfitter's store and come out with a tent, a stove, a pair of boots, enough freeze-dried meals for a week, and a full set of camping dishes...and the weight of all of it combined might not equal that of the little plastic credit card that was used to buy it. The sad news is that now the debt load is heavy. I have a feeling this wife saw her husband's propensity for a lack of control over his "wants" and would love to see him "lighten up" on his lust for weightlessness.

❑ *You spend more money on hunting than I ever do on shopping! You forget to add up the gas, food, corn, dues, and supplies for every trip!* (Wife of a bowhunter)

Let me translate this woman's sentence for some of you city slickers. First, by "shopping," she does not mean going to the store for groceries and other household necessities. When she mentions "gas, food, corn, dues, and supplies," she is referring to…*gas* for the trips to the hunting ground, *food* for the entire weekend at the camp, *corn* for baiting the deer, *dues* refers to hunting licenses, and the word "every" means he goes hunting more than just a few times each season.

❑ *Why does it cost so much to hunt? Why do you have to have more than one gun?* (Wife of a deer hunter)

It is very clear that this woman notices how much venison *really* costs. Annie is aware of it too. I went hunting in Wyoming a few years ago, and my discerning wife counted up the price tag for my 200-pound mule deer that yielded about 80 pounds of meat. Considering the flights, the license, the new rifle I just had to have, and the long list of other little things needed to complete the trip, she came up with around $43.75 per pound. So the answer to why it costs so much to hunt is simple. *Women know how to do math!* Guys, if we would have just married a gal who failed in school at arithmetic, we'd not have so much trouble! As for the number of guns a fellow needs, the answer to that question is easy as well. Most fellows have two trigger fingers. Good grief…give me a hard question to answer!

❑ *Fine!* (Her husband loves sport-related competitions in the video game world)

Okay…I've heard the word "fine" before. A wife can say it in two distinct ways. One has a connotation that is peaceful and agreeable. When heard in this way, it is usually said softly with a vocal delivery that goes from mid-range to a lower calm, almost sexy in tone. My guess is this is how this lady meant to write her response...I hope.

But be warned, there is another way *fine* can be said. It is in a high-pitched, somewhat quick manner with a very strong emphasis on the letter "f," followed by a quick turn on the heels and a huffed departure from the room. When said in this way, *fine* is basically the sound of the sizzle of fire on a really short fuse. More often than not, when *fine!* is the last word in an argument about money spent on a hobby, a fellow can safely assume he is the loser. May we husbands treat our wives in a way that whenever we hear her say the word "fine," it does not resemble the sound that precedes an explosion!

❏ *If you can spend money on hot rod magazines, why can't you spend money on home decorating or parenting magazines for me?* (Wife of someone who likes hot rods)

I couldn't have said it better myself! Really...I couldn't.

❏ *Is there any way you could spread the spending out over the entire year, rather than in the last three months of the year?* (Wife of a deer hunter!)

Being an avid hunter who also works full-time, I know this husband's dilemma. Around early September, when the tree leaves first begin to wilt and that telltale chill in the air sends the thrill of the soon coming opening day of hunting season up his work-weary spine, the husband starts to gather his autumn wits. All year long he has been caught up in making a living (or killing—depending on his level of need or ambition), and now his desire to go hunting becomes nearly overwhelming. Consequently, while he works at his real job with his hands, in his mind he is making a list of all the things he must do to ready himself for the first hunt.

On that list are equipment repairs, replacements, additions, tags, arrows, broadheads, bullets, black powder, camouflage clothing, and a host of other things that require cash to obtain. His wife doesn't understand that what he is dealing with is, in reality, a chemical imbalance in his brain. It's a mysterious hormone that is secreted when the stored adrenaline that accompanies the memories of last year's harvests are mixed with the adrenaline that comes with the thoughts and hopes of this year's shots. In truth, the man cannot control his reaction to it.

Of course, everyone knows who is to blame for this male medical malady. It's the government's fault! Don't they know that marriages could be saved if the wild game commissions in each state would allow deer season year round? If that were the case, hunters would not fall prey to the damaging effects of such a concentrated chemical imbalance that afflicts us in the latter part of each year!

Fortunately for this guy, his wife is not complaining about his spending; she's only challenging his timing. What a glorious gift she is giving him. A crisis has never been so easy to fix. May all husbands who hunt, fish, golf, ski, motorcycle, or hike be as fortunate.

The Good News

The comments I've just shared represent only a few of the wives who were willing to candidly express their concerns about their men and *their* money. However, not all of the questionnaire statements were negative.

I was frankly amazed at the number of very positive words about husbands that were included. What follows is a few of them, and I encourage each man who reads these to consider them as rays of hope for your own quest for helping your wife not resent what you love to do. Also, keep in mind that even though the ladies are writing the words, some of these comments can ultimately be credited to the men who are obviously "doing it right." As a reminder, the questionnaire asked: *If you could say one thing to him about money spent for his hobby/interest, what would you say?*

❑ *Go for it, Babe. You enjoy it, so go do it. If it makes you happy, it'll make me happy.* (Her husband enjoys golf and fishing) What sweeter words could a man hear?

❑ *Thank you for not being excessive in spending our money and for telling me what you are going to buy.* (He fishes, hunts, and motorcycles)

Note the words "our money." Her feelings are obvious. While some guys would say that this husband is whipped, I would argue that he's wise!

❑ *I am so thankful that you are frugal and would never play golf or fish if it put your family's financial needs in a bind.* (A wife of yet another gentleman who likes hearing things hit the water)

Can you feel the gratitude flowing from this woman? It makes me want to go buy a set of Ping clubs and a Ranger Bass boat just so I'll be able to hear Annie say the same thing!

❑ *At least he isn't doing drugs or spending money on other women, and he seems happy.* (He's a hunter and very possibly he is also a hypnotist)

Like a lot of hunters/husbands, I've used the familiar line before to defend my habit. The deal is, I'm thinking that this lady has heard the defense so many times that she is under some sort of spell. While I include this positive comment as just that, I have to concede that some of you are whispering the word "Stepford" at this moment! The fact is, this guy is doing something right...and its not drugs and loose women...that's for sure.

❑ *I see your deer hunting as beneficial to the entire family. You are supplying a great food source that lasts all year long. Thank you!* (I wonder what outdoor activity this guy likes to do!)

I don't know about the rest of you, but I have a feeling when this lady says these words to her husband, the needle on his arousal meter slams to the far right and wraps around the stop peg. I can hear him now. "Ooh! Baby! Keep talking dirty to me!" Oh, the sweet verbal rewards of handling the family funds in the right way.

❑ *Dear, you need to spend more. You deserve it!* (He's a softball fanatic)

I'm dead serious. This statement was right there on the pink paper! It shows that if you do it right, you too can hit a home run!

❑ *I hope you have enough money to spend on your hobby but hopefully, you get enough to get through.* (This wife of a hunter also said in response to another question, "He hunts everything")

Since this husband apparently hunts everything that breathes, crawls, flies, or jumps, he is likely fully satisfied and I feel no sorrow for him. The commendable part about his hobby is that he manages to hunt everything, but at the same time he hasn't lost his wife's approval regarding his spending. Some of us should go live under his roof for a while and learn how he does it.

❏ *I know your purchases are not often, but when you do get something, you really do deserve it.* (He's an avid fisherman)

The key compliment from this wife to her angler is, "Your purchases are not too often." When a man can "reel in" his wants,
he's going to land a huge trophy...the respect of his wife.

❏ *I wish you'd go play golf more often, but I know you feel guilty
about spending the money.* (Another hacker husband.)

For this lady to recognize his feelings of guilt about playing
golf, he had to have verbalized them. Do you realize what an
example this duffer is to the rest of us? If we'd express our reservations about spending money on what we love to do and put our
feelings of guilt out on the table for our wives to see, maybe they
wouldn't be so hesitant to write us checks and send us to the "big
boy toy store." This husband has tapped into an idea of genius
proportions: *Grovel today, shop tomorrow.*

❏ *I appreciate you watching what you spend. And I'm grateful
that you discuss major purchases with me first.* (This husband
has a sailboat)

Yes, I watch what I spend. I watch it as it leaves my hand and
disappears into the money monster's mouth at the checkout counter.
This wise guy (said in best of terms without an ounce of jealousy
involved!) is smart enough to collaborate with his honey on the
big stuff. I can guess his relationship with her is sound and will
likely never sink.

❏ *I am always happy to work extra at teaching swimming or
something to send you on your annual elk hunt. I know how
important it is to you.* (This one's obviously a hunter)

This elk-hunting husband is my new hero! Whatever he does, I want to do. This lady's statement is beyond exciting…it's downright erotic. I'm sorry, but I have to go take a cold shower now. I suppose it really is true that when a man wears the sweet cologne of *unselfishness,* it can drive a woman wild!

I hope these very encouraging remarks by some very happy ladies have inspired you in regard to helping your wife appreciate what you love to do. And I trust that you will give the "equal cash" method an honest try. It can yield some very immediate results! An example of this exciting possibility is found in an e-mail I received a few days after returning home from speaking at a hunter's event.

> Mr. Chapman,
>
> I realized last evening that my husband did get your message about equality in spending that you shared at the wild game dinner. Last night he met me at the store to purchase a new suit. He ended up buying two suits. Now, he knew very well that I wanted to get a new dress so he handed me $200 and told me to pick one out. But we women are so adept at shopping that I was able to buy two dresses, one suit, and two blouses with my $200. He really does get it!
>
> *Lorraine*

I close this chapter with some more good news. If a husband enacts the "price-tag doubling" and "the equal cash" methods long enough, there will come a day when it will not be necessary to actually give his wife the "green paper" as proof that he is sincerely concerned about fairness. Because his attitude of equality has been reshaped by the exercise, eventually all he'll need to do is one of two things. He can say something similar to what I say to Annie when I have spent some money or plan to do so on my hobby. I say, "Annie, I just want you to know I got something for myself today. It cost me (*put the figure here*), and now it's your turn!" Or, he can simply control his tongue when she buys something first. Both will work wonders for your marriage.

2

Left on the Highway

S ome men have a passion for hobbies or outdoor adventures that can be enjoyed practically year round. Hikers, campers, mountain climbers, bicyclists, hockey fans, runners, nature photographers, and basketball junkies are just a few of those who can revel in such an advantage. While their restrictions may be minimal, still there is plenty enough challenge for these adventurers when it comes to not making the mistake of squeezing an excessive amount of marital minutes out of the entire calendar. The result of this error can be the regrettable loss of the good will of their wives.

In another category, there are some of us who have interests that are seasonal. These types of activities may be few, but those who love to do them face a very hefty risk in terms of avoiding the unwanted outcome of alienating a wife. Some of these interests have time limitations due to weather, such as snowmobiling, snow skiing, baseball, and golfing (in the northern regions of the country). Other sports are seasonal due to the laws of the land. Perhaps the most common in that classification is hunting.

Whatever the hobbies are that have time and/or weather limitations attached, engaging in seasonal sports often requires a man to pack his participation in them into a limited section of the annual calendar. In my particular favorite passion, I can consume major amounts of time in the woods after opening day of hunting season comes around. While I have managed to overcome the temptation to be unfair with money, attempting to do the same with time has been a harder struggle.

If any sportsman (whether you enjoy seasonal adventures or the all-year-round type), wants to clearly understand how abandoned a wife can feel if he fails to do it right, consider the following true story.

A preacher I met years ago told about the night he and his wife climbed in their car after a Saturday evening service in Flagstaff, Arizona. He had preached in that city and needed to return to Prescott to be in the pulpit at his own church the next morning.

Not too far into the three-hour journey, he asked his wife if she would mind taking over the driving so he could sleep a little while in order to be rested up for preaching the next day. She kindly agreed, and he pulled off the road to trade places with her.

In the darkness of the desert he exited the driver's side and walked around their car. She slid under the steering wheel. The pastor announced to his wife that instead of napping in the front seat, he would clear the backseat so he could lie down. He opened both doors, took their small pieces of baggage and placed them in the front seat and started to climb in. However, just as he was about to get into the car, he suddenly felt "nature" calling him. He decided to take care of the need before they continued down the road.

—

Perhaps to keep the chill of the night from making her uncomfortable, he didn't say a word as he simultaneously closed both doors on his side, and then turned to step out into the desert for a moment. That's when the unthinkable happened!

Because of the intense darkness, and perhaps being a bit too tired to notice or think clearly, his wife promptly drove away. The preacher was left standing in the total blackness of night, yelling in vain as the taillights grew smaller and smaller.

Nearly an hour passed before the wife came to a "T" in the road and was not totally sure which way to turn. She hated to wake him but needed some directions. Reluctantly she looked around to the backseat and spoke. "Sweetheart, I hate to wake you up but...sweetheart?"

Shocked at who she didn't see in the backseat, she quickly pulled off the road knowing she had to go back. But where did she leave him, and how far would she have to go? Because she had no clue about exactly where her husband had been forsaken, she had to drive slowly.

The preacher said it was one of the longest, coldest, scariest nights he had ever spent. Not one car came by until finally, way off in the distance, he could see headlights coming. He related that he detected a certain hue of deep regret in the glow that very slowly grew on the horizon. Finally she returned for her beloved, and their reunion was, to say the least, quite memorable.

What a great story, and what a noteworthy picture of far too many spouses of seasonal sportsmen such as deer hunters! In reality, it doesn't take too long after the opening day passes that the wife of an excessive hunter begins to feel just like that preacher who was left out on the desert. These women feel utterly abandoned, left standing alone in the dark feeling forgotten and somewhat fearful that it may be months before their husbands come back mentally and emotionally. Very often these ladies are humorously referred to as "deer widows." But for some wives, there is nothing funny about that title.

If you have recently detected that your spouse somehow seems distant when it comes to you and your hobby, my fellow sportsman now is the hour for you to do a one-eighty and carefully search the road for the whereabouts of your bride.

Very likely she waits for you to come back to her. Keep in mind that as much as you would like her to come your way on the issue, she may not feel able. It's too dark, she feels cold out on the highway, and there may be a sense of loneliness in her heart that has paralyzed her. Hopefully, for you this is not the case. For some husbands, however, its time to be brave enough to ask for directions. What would the question sound like? It could be worded, "Honey, when it comes to what I enjoy doing, how do you think I'm handling the 'time' thing? Do you think I'm being fair?" (This question is not for the faint of heart. Only the brave will ask it!)

The Good Husband's Principle

Never let your wife feel abandoned

The guideline I suggest that you follow, no matter what you enjoy doing, is very simple: *Strive to do all you can possibly do to never let your wife feel abandoned on the highway of your hobby!* Always remember that in the mind of a wife, feeling second place is feeling no place at all.

Once again, I readily admit my propensity for biting more time off the recreational clock than I should chew. That confession is subtly embodied in the following lyric that I wrote while riding my motorcycle on a Tennessee back road. It was mid-July when I rolled by a mature field of corn. As I looked to my right and saw the tall stand of deep green stalks, it occurred to me, "In just a few weeks the color of the corn will start to change. That means only one thing...deer season is right around the corner!"

I got so pumped in that moment that I found my right hand twisting the throttle just a little further than I normally would… or should. I came to my senses and slowed to the speed limit, smiling at the "hunterholic" thought I had just had. That's when the lyric that follows was born.

The First Winds of Autumn

When the green of the cornstalk
begins to turn brown,
when the time for the goldenrod bloom
comes around,
that's when I look to the hills for I know
soon I'll walk there again
with my arrow and bow.

When the fruit of the white oak
is ready to fall,
and when the hummingbird feels
that old Mexico call,
and when tears touch the cheeks
of my sweetheart she knows
soon it's farewell to her man with
the arrow and bow.

The heart of the hunter who can explain
how the first winds of autumn
seem to whisper my name
and it sends me to dreamin'
'bout the morning I'll go
back up to the hills with my arrow and bow.

When the tender young fawn
is spotted no more,
and their fathers prepare
for their November wars,

I can't help but wonder if the mighty ones know
soon I will come with my arrow and bow.

The heart of the hunter who can explain
how the first winds of autumn
seem to whisper my name
and it sends me to dreamin'
'bout the morning I'll go
back up to the hills with my arrow and bow.[1]

Perhaps some of the lyrical descriptions of a few of the welcomed signs of an approaching season sound familiar to you. If so, you and I probably have much in common. Maybe you, as well as your wife, can especially relate to the lines that say, "...and when tears touch the cheeks / of my sweetheart she knows / soon it's farewell to her man / with the arrow and bow."

If this is the case, I should admit that while those lines might hold just a bit of humor, they are in reality a gut-wrenching, honest confession of a very real weakness I have. I, like many husbands with a seasonally affected hobby, struggle with being fair to my wife in the area of time consumed while hunting.

Thankfully, when I did ask Annie how I was doing with the balance of time, she was candid enough to point out the fact that somewhere along the way I had taken a wrong turn. Since that day, I have been consciously working at helping her to not resent the time I spend outdoors.

Do I resent her challenge? No way! Like an old mature turkey, I may be ugly but I'm not stupid. I took it as clear proof that Annie loved me enough to give me a straightforward answer in order to help me love her better. Quite frankly, the trophy of her acceptance is a lot bigger than any that can be found in the woods.

Equal Time

"Hold your lover's hands…hold the hands of time…feel them both pulling away." In other words, the motion of the fleeting years cannot be stopped. Nor can we expect those we love to be with us always. This truth alone is plenty enough reason for a husband to treat his wife with kindness, especially in the area of how much of the day he consumes for himself and how much of it he gives to her. It might help for a man to remember that all clocks come with even numbers, making it much easier to share time equally with her.

Under the heading of maintaining the wise rule of giving her "equal time," I offer the following tip to any husband who is courageous enough to admit he is overdoing the doing. I do it for the sake of the quality of your marriage and for the purpose of helping you regain her trust in your sense of direction. Keep in mind that to attempt this idea will be a bit like bench-pressing 200 pounds. Basically, it's a simple thing to do, but in no way is it easy because it requires a courageous defiance of our human tendency to be self-centered. Here's the idea: If you want to help your wife not resent the time you spend doing your favorite thing…earn your leisure time!

> **The Good Husband's Principle**
>
> **Earn your leisure time**

What do I mean by "earn your leisure"? If you know you want to spend three or four hours unwinding in a tree stand, a duck blind, a bass boat, on a fairway, or on a ski slope, then give your wife equal time to do the same. You can do so in a lot of ways, but the two I use most often is helping Annie with something she wants to get done and giving her equal time away from home to do something she likes to do.

Keep in mind that this method always works better if you give her equal time *up front*. Promising to do something with (or for) her *after* you have spent time on your interest can put you in the dangerous position of forgetting to follow through. If, however you choose to *owe* your wife some equal time, be sure to keep your promise. Otherwise you'll end up like the abandoned preacher in Arizona. And if you think it can be frigid out on a dark desert highway, remember there's nothing colder than a wife's resentful shoulder.

I readily admit that for some men, giving their wives equal time may seem impossible. Work schedules, church and social activities, and a list of other commitments may make the "equal time" method seem like too tall a mountain to climb. Your despair is noted. I am personally familiar with the upward trek, just like a friend who recently sent me the following e-mail. I asked him how he was doing with the time issue, and he wrote:

> My problem is my addictive "involvaholic" personality. The school board needs a Christian man, the ministerial alliance needs someone to run the thrift shop on Saturday, the church van needs the tires rotated, and some kids across town need to be picked up for Wednesday night youth service. And don't forget that a good Christian Senate hopeful will be needing someone from the district to introduce him and maybe coordinate his campaign in the area….To these, I have had trouble saying no!
>
> But with my wife, I haven't done as well. She says something like "Come let me show you how well Digo (one of our horses) is doing." I say, "I don't have the time." That's been a disappointment for her. But there's good news. That has/is changing. I am basically learning to say "No" to more of other people's requests and "Yes" to most of hers.
>
> Here's the awesome thing I've learned. When a husband submits to changing and his wife sees he really does love her more than the time bandits that attack a marriage,

she then lovingly wants him to go and "have a good time." Or, maybe she just gets sick of me being around. Either way, things are improving around our house now that I'm on the right track.

Thanks for asking,

Dan

Like Dan, whose wife is benefiting by his ongoing efforts to improve, I too have felt the joy of the matrimonial bliss seen in Annie's eyes when I'm doing the "time thing" right. For the sake of regaining your wife's good will, I urge you to think in terms of fairness with her, even if it means sacrificing your needs from time to time.

To give you an idea of how it can be done, here's an example of how it works in my own marriage. Through the years Annie and I have engaged in a friendly rivalry. We are always trying to out serve each other. It is a contest (for lack of a better word) that has its roots in a specific instruction found in the Holy Scriptures. In the second chapter of Philippians in the New King James Version of the Bible, under the heading of "Unity Through Humility," verse number four offers the following admonition: "Let each of you look out not only for his own interests, but also for the interests of others."

Before you lose heart and think you have to completely give up your hobby, take note that the passage does not deny or reduce the value of your personal interests. Instead, it simply points out that choosing to view the other person's interests as equally important to your own is a key to living in harmony with people...and especially with your wife!

Though this passage is directed to all those who make up the church, when Annie and I began applying the principle to our marriage, everything changed. It was not long after doing so that we began to call the contest our "romantic competition." It has actually been fun to try to outdo each other when it comes to the romance of serving.

Each year in the springtime I am presented with one of the absolute best opportunities to outserve my wife and earn some time in the woods. Annie has a beautiful garden in our backyard. Amazingly, about the time the cold winter ground begins to thaw in the warmth of the March and April sun in Tennessee, and as the tender sprouts of plants and flowers begin to burst through the softening dirt, something else glorious begins. The turkey gobblers start gobbling.

Talk about a conflict! Where would I rather be? Helping Annie mulch and weed the garden or trying to outsmart an old tom turkey? If I answer honestly, in some guys' minds I risk sounding like what actor and California Governor Arnold Shwartzenegger calls a "girlie man." But being secure in my manhood, I will be honest. *I like doing both!*

I find a great deal of enjoyment in doing things for Annie such as hauling and spreading manure-tainted mulch, carrying the bug-infested brushy remains of last year's growth off to the dump, and pulling unwanted weeds until my poor trigger finger(s) bleed. I love it.

I especially like to fulfill her request of helping her keep the critters away from her flowers. Rabbits, squirrels, and gophers are menaces that don't appreciate my hunter's skills. But I don't stop there. I even went to Montana once and eliminated a big old black bear that I just knew was going to migrate to Tennessee someday and find Annie's garden. It was a sacrifice on my part, but I did it just for her!

Why do I like to do these things? One, Annie really appreciates it. Two, it helps me *earn* guilt-free time in the woods. When I go turkey hunting *after* I have been careful to spend time helping

Annie with her gardening needs, then I can chase the springtime gobblers without that nagging feeling that Annie may be resenting what I'm doing.

Warning!

To my fellow hunters and to all fans of seasonal and nonseasonal sports, I offer this caution. Doing "good deeds" for your wife in one section of the calendar in order to spend unlimited, large blocks of time doing what you love to do during a much later portion of the year may not work effectively. To put it another way, we should not attempt to deposit days, minutes, and hours into the "Husband's Bank of Time" in the summer and then expect to draw it all out in the winter. This method is not likely to work very well. By the time the winter season you've been waiting so long for comes, the currency in your account has plummeted in value. Why is this true? Annie has the answer.

She says, "Most women have short memories when it comes to what a man *did do,* but long memories when it comes to what he *didn't do*." Safely assuming my wise wife is correct in her assessment, a woman (especially if there are small children involved) lives in the present. If you are gone most of the weekdays working, then consistently disappear on the weekends to the woods or streams or to do whatever you enjoy doing, no matter how much you might have done months ago, your wife probably won't take those investments into account. Like it or not, she will be affected most by what you are doing *in the present.* While making deposits into the "Husband's Bank of Time" may work for some, for most of us it may not yield the dividends we hope for.

All husbands with hobbies would be wise to always remember that...

Yesterday (what you did for her last summer) is a *canceled check,*

Tomorrow (what you promise you'll do for her later) is a *promissory note,*

Today is *cash*!

What Other Husbands Say

For the purpose of comforting those who may think they are totally alone in the "equal time" struggle, here are a few comments from husbands who answered the following questions:

Question A: *If there is a problem area (great or small) related to your interest as it pertains to your marriage, can you identify it?*

Question B: *What steps do you plan to take to resolve this conflict?*

The responses are revealing.

- ❑ A) *She is frustrated when she feels like she and the kids are second to hunting.*
- ❑ B) *I plan to ask her what I can do for her to help her have equal time and energy for something of her own.* (He hunts deer and turkey, shoots competitive archery)

This fellow's admission confirms my concern for all husbands with hobbies. His plan for resolution gives me great optimism. I hope that since the day he wrote the words he has followed through. If he did, I have a feeling he's a happier hunter!

- ❑ A) *I never have any personal time to myself.*
- ❑ B) *I want to get her to go with me.* (He loves fly-fishing)

Though his intentions are commendable, this is a classic example of a how one fisherman let the mental line get really tangled. On one hand, he cries out for time alone; on the other, he wants her to go with him. These opposing desires reveal an important insight for all husbands who feel recreationally deprived. When a man says, "I wish she'd go with me," what he often means is, "I wish she'd go so I won't have to feel guilty while I'm out there." He's willing to take her along, even though he'd rather be doing what he loves to do without her. It's irrational, for sure, but the power of guilt can cause a fellow to say and do some really strange things.

While it is awkward to admit, I have been known to put Annie through the pain of taking her with me so I wouldn't feel guilty about being gone. A few years ago, as the closing day of Tennessee's deer season neared, I was anxious to make one final attempt to fill a tag. I knew, however, that I had already been to the woods far too many times during the season. I struggled with the fact that by disappearing from the house for yet another day I might do damage to my reputation as a man of restraint. What did I do? I came up with a brilliant solution to my dilemma. I decided to invite Annie to accompany me to the beauty of the great outdoors.

I was sure she would recognize how considerate it was for me to extend the invitation, and then say, "I can see how much this means to you, but if you don't mind I'll stay here at home. Please...go and enjoy one more outing. It'll do you good." With that answer I would win both ways. My good reputation would remain intact, and I'd get to go hunting too! Was I ever shocked when she agreed to go.

I ended up digging through my boxes of camo to find something she could wear. With the two of us looking quite coordinated in our matching outfits, we entered the woods on a sunny afternoon. She followed me to the huge oak tree at the edge of a green field where I had planned to hunt. I cleared a place on the ground, put a blanket down on the cold forest floor, and the two of us settled in for the vigil.

To understand the marital tragedy that transpired that afternoon, you must be aware that one of the most important things about deer hunting is to be quiet and listen. For the first few minutes that's exactly what we did. However, the silence didn't last long. Annie errantly thought it was a good time to talk. After all, we were alone together, away from the phone and the kids. The setting seemed right for communication between a husband and a wife...at least that's how she saw it.

The subjects that were covered ranged from children to troubled friends to house repairs that needed attention. I tried really hard to hunt, talk, and listen at the same time—and to do so without Annie knowing that I was growing more and more agitated. But I failed miserably. After a little while I succumbed to my frustration and said, "Babe, if we're going to see any deer today, we can't be talking!"

Boy, did that work. Not another word was said...not one...not for the rest of the afternoon. And I could tell by the frigid air that hung between us that I had really goofed up.

As we headed home (with an empty tag and a wounded "dear"), Annie finally spoke up. "Steve, I could have stayed home and not talked. I thought you wanted me to go with you so we could have some time together. Sitting on the cold ground and being quiet was not quite what I had in mind."

I never tried that stunt again. Nor do I recommend it to anyone else.

❏ A) *We don't spend enough quality time together.*

❏ B) *Find something besides riding that we can do together.* (Motorcyclist)

Here is a rare bird of the good kind. When I read this husband's assessment, my hope in husbandkind was renewed. I happen to know him personally, and he understands an important, undeniable truth: "*Quantity* time leads to *quality* time" or "People spell love T-I-M-E." Also, I know he's smart enough that when he eventually finds that other "something" to do with his wife, it will not be an activity like sitting in a deerstand all day in the blistering cold or wrestling alligators in a Florida swamp. It will be something *she* truly enjoys.

❏ A) *I would like to go out on my sailboat more than I do.*

❏ B) *Talk about it.* (Sailing is his passion)

Obviously, he feels terribly underprivileged in the time he gets to sail. However, the waters are looking calmer because he has wisely put his boat on the right course. Talking with his wife about his longing for time on the sea will lead to some smooth sailing.

❏ A) *It takes time away from us.*

❏ B) *Get a side car!* (Another biker)

I really like this guy. His confession that his hobby "takes time away from us" is not an easy thing to admit. We can all admire his nerve. For those of us who love the rumble of the iron beast, the solution for giving his wife equal time is….well…genius? It's probably not going to work, but it's truly a brilliant idea.

❏ A) *She likes to keep our schedule full. She has done better at checking with me especially about late October and November commitments.*

❏ B) *Let her know well in advance when I'd like to be in the woods.* (An archery season hunter)

This is obviously a reverse of the typical situation. Generally a husband might not be the one who shows a willingness to work around his mate's itinerary. But this fellow is wise in offering to let her know in advance when he'd like to enter the woods. A serious student of the behavior of the habits of deer can predict with some reasonable accuracy when the hottest time might be for hunting rut-active bucks in his territory. This knowledge will serve him well because he can let his wife know prior to opening of season when he'd like to go. The result could be the resolution of a lot of conflicts with the calendar.

❑ A) *My wife might feel put out with the time I spend doing what I love, but rarely will she express it or show it.*

❑ B) (*No response*)

There may be a reason she doesn't say anything. I'm not giving this husband the benefit of the doubt because I know a few "time-hogging" guys whose wives have shut down in the area of communication. I think I can make a reasonably intelligent guess at what the problem might be. She may have tried in the past to express her feelings but never saw the light come on in his eyes. She may have given up. The next chapter addresses the issue connected to this husband's possible dilemma. It involves the dreaded "C" word. If you dare…turn the page.

3

The "C" Word

I have seen the dreaded "C" word cause husbands' faces to twitch nervously. When Annie or I mention the word at the concerts and seminars we conduct for married couples, I have watched men shift in their seats like a dentist was coming at them with a high-powered Black & Decker drill. What is the "C" word?

Communication!

I remain appreciative of the description I heard years ago of the act of communicating. It was teacher Chuck Snyder who said, "Communication...it's kind of like vomiting...you don't want to do it but it feels so good when you get it over with." Not everyone would readily embrace Chuck's statement as an accurate definition of the process of interacting with a spouse. But I find it refreshing. The imagery embodied in the quip has, through the years, helped me "bring up" thoughts and feelings that I may not have otherwise been capable or willing to share with Annie. I know she has been grateful for Mr. Snyder's wisdom and would not want me to hurl it out of my psyche. Now I throw it up on the screen of your mind for your consideration. Please don't toss it away like stale cookies.

I realize there are a lot of unavoidable hazards on the road to good marital communication. The urgent needs of a couple's economy, their kids, their extended family concerns, and community issues are just a few of the attention-consuming cares of life. But not all hazards on the verbal highway are unintentional. Some are placed in our way by our own hands.

The Good Husband's Principle

Communicate!

This can be especially true for those of us who have a serious passion for our various recreational vices. Some guys view them as antidotes for the ailment of stress or the salve that will cure the itch for solitude. Then there are some who are addicted to the drug of adrenaline that can be extracted from the more risky hobbies such as skydiving and race-car driving. Whatever the reason is for clinging to our obsessions, if we value the good favor of our wives, we will not allow our hobbies to become roadblocks to communicating with her.

Why Leads to How

If you are wondering why communication is so important to your wife, then I am very happy to announce to you that you are halfway there in finding success as a communicative husband. This is true because if a man knows *why* something should be done, more than likely he'll figure out *how* to do it. For example, as a young husband who had absolutely no home-repair skills to speak of, I clearly remember the day when I discovered *how* to change a wax gasket in a commode assembly. It came about because I discovered *why* there was water standing on our apartment floor. So to help you understand why your wife needs you to figure out how to talk and listen to her, I offer you an important...why.

Drawing from the wisdom of the book of Proverbs, verse 18:21 NASB, hear these words: "Death and life are in the power of the tongue...." Look at the positive side of this passage. The word "life" (*chayah* in the original language) implies the idea of preserving, refreshing, rebuilding, and restoring to life. When we communicate with our wives consistently, effectively, and wisely, we are literally pouring energy and vitality into her soul. When we fail to feed her appetite for verbal interaction, we fall short of meeting her need for emotional nourishment. Eventually, death could come to the relationship—an outcome none of us want.

If you don't think the power of life is in the human tongue, consider this scenario. Suppose you are a coal miner trapped alone deep below the surface of the ground. Your fate seems sealed by the rubble that blocks the passageways to fresh air. Days have gone by, and you're about to give up. Suddenly you hear the muffled, distant sound of voices. You realize that rescuers have come to save you! In that moment, wouldn't your very spirit fill with new vigor— enough to help you hold on until you see the light of day again? You bet! It is then that you would understand the undeniable power of life that can be found in the sound of the human voice.

From time to time, when we fail to keep the lines of communication open with our wives, they may feel like trapped miners. Some ladies may have even given up on ever hearing the refreshing and renewing sound of their husbands' voices. But it's not too late for a rescue.

What follows are some guidelines to help you stay in touch with your wife. These ideas will help you dig through the rubble of your silence and, at last, recover the emotional life of your bride. For others, these suggestions might simply ensure that the collapse never happens.

Some How To's

Now that you understand at least one reason *why* your wife needs you to talk to her, I offer a few *hows* to help you follow through with the rescue. The number one recommendation I submit for how to help your wife see that you have not had a total lobotomy or that your cat is not chewing on your tongue is to *avoid being overly distracted by your interest.*

As an avid…nearly rabid…fan of hunting the incredibly intelligent and ellusive whitetail deer, I deal with the very real and present danger of allowing myself far too much thought about the pursuit. It is not uncommon for Annie to attempt to get my attention only to find me in an impenetrable trance on the couch as yet another hunting video plays on our television. She knows that unless blood is flowing from the wound of a loved one who needs my attention or an IRS agent is at the door, I don't want to be disturbed. It is in moments like these that hunting has not just come too close to home, it has taken over the home.

The Good Husband's Principle

Avoid being overly distracted by your interest

Another place that can reveal my penchant for ignoring my wife's voice can be while riding in the car with her. The problem is not that I don't want to talk with her. The dilemma is that when we're in the car, we are usually riding in the out of doors! The highways of our rural region of the country are not just paved passages from one town to the next. Many of them are vantage points for hunters. A fellow never knows what roadside meadow might hold a herd of deer; therefore, he must always be on the alert!

The trouble with this strange preoccupation with animal sightings is usually not realized until it's too late. It might happen in this way for you: You're driving through an area that you know holds great promise for whitetail sightings. The fields are ripe with the tasty growth of alfalfa or mature soybeans. The time is 4:30, and you know that the deer have likely left their bedding areas and are headed to open feeding grounds.

With the eyes of a hawk you scan the edges of the meadows as you pass them at 55 miles per hour. Here's where the trouble comes in: Your level of concentration on picking out the familiar brown fur is so high that you fail to hear your wife talking. Like so many men, the more you see the less you hear. Consequently, in your mind her voice sounds like a radio that has been wrapped in a bed mattress.

What you also don't know is that she has just asked you a question that may well have been on her mind for years. She asks, "Sweetheart, were you ever seriously involved with anyone else before you met me and asked me to marry you?"

In the same instant that she is asking you such a loaded question, you suddenly see a group of deer in a field off to your right. Because you are driving like a "buckaholic" and are completely focused on the herd, you do not recognize that you are looking right over the bridge of your wife's nose. It appears to her that you are looking her right in the eyes as you respond, "Oh, Babe, there's at least nine or ten of 'em...pretty ones, too!" Without even knowing it, you've just run off of Happily Married Road and crashed into the "I shouldn't have said that" tree.

I could probably offer you some sort of clinically based solution approved by the board of directors of the School for the Advancement of Proper Male Psychological Behavior. However, the answer for avoiding these kinds of fatal fixations is really not complicated at all. Just don't do it, Bubba! It's simple...but it's not easy. Remember, if you know the *why*, you'll do the *how*.

Here are some other *hows* for a husband with a passion who wants to effectively communicate with his wife:

Don't give her clouds and wind without the rain. This wisdom also comes from the book of Proverbs, chapter 25, verse 14. The picture in this verse is well understood by any farmer. He looks to his fields that are dry and thirsty for moisture. Then the sky suddenly fills with clouds, and the trees begin to sway with the wind. These are exciting signs that a much-needed rainstorm may be brewing. His hopes are up, yet the clouds pass, the wind lays low again, and the rain never falls. Nature has disappointed him, and his fields remain thirsty.

> **The Good Husband's Principle**
>
> **Don't give her clouds and wind without the rain**

When we promise with our words that we will come home at a certain hour after enjoying our habit, and we don't show up at that time, we have given her clouds and wind. When we say we will reduce the amount of time we are "out there," but then make no effort to do so, to her it's clouds and wind. Get the point? How can she find life and hope in your words if they never produce?

Don't put her in "the pit." The psalmist David said to the Lord, "My rock, do not be deaf to me, for if You are be silent to me, I will become like those who go down to the pit" (Psalm 28:1 NASB). The "pit" in biblical times was usually a dry cistern used for a prison. David knew that God's silence would say something to him he didn't want to know. That is, that the Almighty would no longer be present to help in time of need or to hear the man when he cried out for rescue from his pursuers. Without the Lord's nearness and His intervention, when David lifted his voice in despair he knew his destiny was the dreaded pit.

> **The Good Husband's Principle**
>
> **Don't put her in the pit**

A husband's silence can say a great deal to a wife: *I don't care; I don't feel close to you; I will not be there for you when you cry for help.* If your mate feels like she has been dropped into the pit of your silence, it's time for you to lift her up using the rescuing hand of your kind words.

The "got to/get to" rule. A local pastor explained this conflict of feelings in this way. He said he has heard members say to him, "I've *got* to go to early service this Sunday because I *get* to go to the Titans' football game at noon." The former was considered a duty; the latter was seen as a pleasure. The pastor lamented that he hoped that all of his members might someday feel the reverse of the got to/get to principle in regard to church attendance.

When it comes to communicating with our wives, we should always try to make her feel like it is something that we "get" to do. Believe me, she'll detect it if you are interacting with her because you feel like you have "got" to do it. How can you regain the "get to" if you've lost it? One thing I do is to remember to see her as God sees her.

> **The Good Husband's Principle**
>
> **I "get to" spend time with my wife**

In the apostle Peter's writings, he refers to woman as a "weaker vessel" (1 Peter 3:7 NKJV). While this may refer to the fact that typically her physical strength may not be as great as that of the man, I lean to another image that can be drawn from this word picture. The woman is like a fine, priceless work of art. Perhaps a vase that may be dainty in form, but there is no measure when it comes to its incredible value. If I see my wife as our Creator sees her; that is "priceless," then my perception of her worth changes. If that is true, I will no longer consider my communication with her as a "got to" but as a "get to!"

If I read further in the verse, I discover that when I talk to Annie I am not just talking to a woman but ultimately I am conversing with a fellow heir in the grace of life. That sobering reality changes everything.

One other note about that passage: The very last line of verse seven offers me one of the greatest promises a man can rely upon. The entire verse in the New American Standard Bible reads,

> You husbands in the same way, live with your wives in an understanding way, as with someone weaker [a weaker vessel], since she is a woman; and show her honor as a fellow heir of the grace of life, so that your prayers will not be hindered.

Do you see what I see? Husbands, if we expect to be able to communicate with God through prayer, then one of the first things we must do is live with our wives in an understanding way. The logical conclusion is a question: How will we ever understand our wives if we don't talk to them? The lyric that follows could very well describe the desire of your wife's heart. If it does, may God give you the courage to remove any roadblocks to communicating with her...even if the hazard is your hobby.

Will You Talk to Me?

I look into your eyes
I try to read your mind
'Cause I just want to know
What's on your heart sometimes.
There must be some words
You just want to set free.
Baby, will you talk to me?

They say silence is golden
Maybe that's true,
But not when it comes
To me and you.
Just your whisper
Is like a good rain,
But it's a desert
When you don't speak.
Baby, will you talk to me?

Talk to me.
Talk to me.
And I promise I will listen
Quietly.
You have the words,
I have the need.
Baby, will you talk to me?

The heart is a room
Where the thoughts are stored,
And the tongue
Will unlock that door.
I will wait for you
To turn that key.
Baby, will you talk to me?[2]

BUSINESS REPLY MAIL

FIRST-CLASS MAIL   PERMIT NO 181   FLAGLER BEACH FL

POSTAGE WILL BE PAID BY ADDRESSEE

EQUUS

SUBSCRIPTION DEPARTMENT
PO BOX 420078
PALM COAST FL 32142-8552

NO POSTAGE
NECESSARY
IF MAILED IN THE
UNITED STATES

EQUUS

Subscriber's Privilege Certificate

This certificate entitles bearer to receive EQUUS
at a savings of over $83 off the newsstand price.

☐ 12 issues just $24 - Save $35! ☐ 24 issues just $36 - Save $83!

Name _____

Address _____

City/State/Zip _____

E-mail _____ To contact you about your subscription, events and special offers. 68ESEB
☐ Bill me ☐ Payment enclosed

Satisfaction guaranteed or your money back.

Savings based on annual newsstand price of $59.88.

4

Home Alone

I'll never forget the sound of our friend's nervous voice when I answered her phone call. Skipping right over my standard greeting or any of the usual chitchat, she quickly and nervously asked, "Is Annie there?" The mother of four kids all under the age of five waited for my response to her abrupt inquiry. Assuming that there might have been some kind of turmoil at her residence, I answered, "No, Annie has gone to the store. What's going on over at your house?"

She reported, "Mandy [her four-year old daughter] just ate a stupid cricket."

I didn't think the news merited the level of alarm in her voice, so I attempted to soothe the frazzled mom with a little humor. I was sure that if I delivered it with an unruffled and confident tone it would provide all the comfort she needed at the moment. "Oh, don't worry about the cricket. I've heard that missionaries all around the world have eaten those things many times through the years. They may be crunchy, but they're full of protein."

I heard nothing but the anxious sound of labored breathing on the other end. I could sense that my attempt at calming her with a little wit did not quite do its intended job. Her next words told me that the situation was more serious than I thought.

"Yes, but this cricket was floating in insecticide!"

My concern for her and her child suddenly kicked into high gear, so I did what I thought was best. I added another funny.

"Well, she'll glow in the dark now. You won't have to search so hard for her at night!"

Was that ever dumb. I didn't even get a courtesy chuckle from her. My "stand up" had fallen. All she said was a desperate, "What in the world am I going to do? Jack is at work, and I can't reach him!"

Finally realizing that the need was urgent, I gave the best advice I could give to a frightened mother. "You better get that girl to an emergency room right away!"

I'm happy to report that the outcome was good. The cricket, being already deceased, did not suffer at all from the ivory crushing. As far as the little girl is concerned, other than finding her on occasion behind her parents' couch rubbing her legs together and making strange, relentless high-pitched noises, she seems fine. I noticed the next day that she was having a hopping good time with her siblings in the backyard.

However, her mother didn't fair as well. The cricket episode was almost more than her tired mind could handle. She was in need of a huge break. The problem is that as far as I know, it never happened.

The story I just told you is true, except, of course, the part about the kid making strange noises behind the couch. The plight of the mom represents the predicament a lot of mothers face, including the wives of the men who are the focus of this book. A dad with hobbies who wants to win his wife's ongoing favor toward the thing he likes to do will make sure that she gets her share of down time without the kids. Any father who would think for a moment that this is not necessary reveals that he has a brain the size of a…well… a cricket.

Closely related to the previous chapters about being fair with cash and time and effectively communicating with your wife is the matter of helping with the load involved with raising kids. Truthfully, this need is so obvious

> **The Good Husband's Principle**
>
> **Give your wife some responsibility-free down time**

that I seriously considered not including it on the list of helpful tips. Yet there are some guys who are so keyed in to their own interest that they struggle to see the need their wives have for some physical and emotional relief from the rigors of momhood. For that reason, I must challenge you to make sure you're being fair and doing it right when it comes to helping your wife carry the weight of your kids.

The Decision

Back in 1977, when our firstborn came along, life sure did change for Annie and me. No longer were we the carefree couple who could do just about anything we wanted with our time. Those days ended with what one new father called "the cutting of the *unbiblical* cord." Our time became our only begotten son's time, and that was fine with us. We loved him then, and we love him even more today. But for a dedicated hunter, having to change the schedule so drastically was a tough challenge to face.

Then in 1980, our daughter, Heidi, was born. We couldn't have been more delighted. By then I was enjoying being a dad so much that the sting of having to reduce the number of trips to the woods so drastically was really not that painful. However, the desire to enjoy the outdoors remained.

Though I had an occasional opportunity to hunt, as well as to do other outdoor things that I enjoyed such as fish, camp, canoe, and bicycle, I resigned myself to the likelihood that going with the regularity I longed for might never happen again. But as the kids started getting a little older and able to walk a little farther and endure some of the challenges that nature can throw at humans (cold, bugs, the dark of night), I began to see a ray of hope.

It was about that time that I made a conscious decision that became one of the very best I ever made. I decided that instead of abandoning the kids in order to enjoy the great outdoors, I would introduce them to the things I loved to do and see if any of them would pique their interest. As I relate a few of these stories, keep in mind that I am doing so in the context of helping you as a husband be a help to your wife in regards to not resenting what you enjoy doing. On that basis, see if you can find the two hidden treasures that I found while including my kids in my interests.

Things That Go Boom!

When Nathan was less than ten years old, I sought his mother's approval about taking him into the hunter's woods with me. I knew without a doubt that she would have issues with her youngster being around devices that go boom. I was aware of this because I distinctly remember the day when our son was just a little guy and Annie anxiously asked, "Are you ever going to get Nathan one of those 21's?"

I had to think for a second about what she was asking. Then it dawned on me that she was referring to a .22 caliber rifle. I smiled understandably and responded, "Maybe someday." Based on the reservations that I knew Annie had about guns, I wanted to make sure that Nathan and I had her blessing to go hunting together. Thankfully, she expressed her confidence in my sense of safety and agreed to permit her tender little boy to accompany me on his first squirrel hunt. (When we look back on that day, Nathan and I are convinced that her decision to grant us favor was not at all influenced by us begging and crying in the prostrate position at her feet!)

I didn't let Nathan handle a weapon on that first hunt. I feared that if I let him put my 12-gauge shotgun to his shoulder and pull the trigger, the gun would kick him so hard that it would take meat on both ends. We agreed that I would do all the blasting. However, he did sit right beside me during the hunt. To say the least, it was quite an educational day for my boy. We ended up with a couple of bushytails for the frying pan.

Knowing that hunting has its inherent emotional downside in terms of taking the life of unsuspecting creatures, I made a necessary determination in advance. If Nathan revealed a consistent hesitance about "harvesting" food in such a way, I would not force him to continue following me on the trail of my love for hunting. This policy had its roots in a truth that is hard for some men to accept. Simply, *you don't have to hunt to be a man, and you don't have to be a man to hunt.* (The later part of this quip will especially encourage dads who love to hunt and who have daughters!) While I was more than willing to allow Nathan the freedom to reject the activity of hunting, I have to admit that I hoped he would take to the idea. Fortunately, he did just that.

Not too long after our first trip to the woods together, we both attended the hunter's safety course. I had not yet attended the seminar, and doing so with my son was pure fun. Both of us passed our tests with no trouble at all. Since that day we have enjoyed plenty of "stand time." Also, the trips in the truck, the nights in hunting cabins, the journeys out west to pursue elk and mule deer, and many other opportunities to be side by side that are unique to the world of hunting have yielded some incredible memories. These moments are cherished treasures in our hearts and minds.

Being with my son in the great outdoors didn't stop when we exited the woods. We engaged in other favorite adventures that were just as exciting. We've played a few rounds of golf. We discovered that golf is a lot like hunting in that we ended up in the woods looking for something. Parts of the Appalachian Trail contain a fair number of our footprints. The fish in the Gulf of Mexico are a little fatter today because we feed them from time to time…and a few of them fed us! We've stood at attention side by side in the stands to honor the heart-pounding, ear-throbbing, first full lap speed pass of a field of cars at NASCAR events. We've even driven officially sanctioned race cars at breakneck speeds around the Charlotte Speedway in North Carolina.

Of all the outdoor activities we have enjoyed together, hunting remains our favorite connection. However, there is one other adventure that stands out as one of the most memorable. It continues to be a favorite of mine because so much was taught as a result of the experience.

Because I wanted to teach Nathan the importance of setting a goal and staying with it until it is accomplished, I chose to include him on a long-dreamed-of bicycle trip from Nashville to West Virginia. He was around 15 years old and fully capable of enduring the nearly 500 miles of hills and highways.

The journey was unbelievable. It's quite interesting how pain and bonding go together. We were both hurting and happy the whole way. One very memorable moment we both will never forget happened in Kentucky.

> We had climbed a steep hill on a secluded back road in central Kentucky. When we reached the top we were barely rolling, and both of us were panting for breath. As we crested the hill, just before we began the relief of the descent, I looked across the yard to my right and saw a little white frame house sitting about 75 yards off the road.

It had a high front porch and underneath it was a group of dogs. Because of the bank of the road, I was eye level with the critters and all they could possibly have seen was our heads bobbing along. Still, they stood up and took off toward us the instant they caught sight of us. All of them. The thought of the carnage they were about to create was frightening. Instinctively I yelled to Nathan, "Get your Halt ready and prepare to sprint. (Halt is a biker's self-defense pepper spray designed for dogs.)

The barking beasts came off the bank and onto the road. For some reason they ignored me and darted in front of Nathan. In the excitement of the moment, he shot a stream of pepper spray over his handlebars, straight at the dogs. He was peddling for his life and didn't realize that his forward motion would carry him directly into the residual orange mist that hung in the air. In essence, he had just maced himself. Instantly he began to gasp and grabbed for his face with both hands, leaving the handlebars at the mercy of the road. Off into the ditch he went.

What happened next was remarkable. I assumed that both of us were about to become Kibbles and Bits. Instead, all three of the dogs rushed over to Nathan. As he wiped at the pepper-induced tears and scrambled to get up off the ground, he discovered that the dogs had stopped short of where he had fallen. They just stood there staring at him as if they were apologetic for causing the accident. They seemed to want to comfort the unfortunate stranger. Nathan quickly maneuvered his uninjured bike onto its wheels and, although the road was a blur, he rode on, (mumbling things under his breath he didn't want me to hear). We were both glad to still be among the living.

What an adventure we had. One thing I told Nathan before we left Tennessee was that the sign we would look for that our long trip was nearly over was the familiar "big blue bridge." Our destination was his grandparent's house in the town of Point Pleasant, West Virginia, and we both knew that the blue-painted structure would be the last quarter mile we would pedal before reaching our goal. On the way, we talked frequently about the joy we would feel when we had gone far and long enough to see the "big blue bridge" in the distance. That exchange often took place when our derrieres were protesting the abuse.

We finally did see the bridge, and we arrived in Point Pleasant, but it was not without fanfare. Having advance notice of the estimated day and time of arrival, my dad had asked the local newspaper to show up and take pictures (which they used for a front-page report about our adventure in the following day's issue). He had also arranged for a police escort from the end of the blue bridge all the way through town. It couldn't have been more exciting!

As a father who wanted to teach his son the importance of following through on commitment, I wondered if the grueling trip had accomplished my goal. Three years later I realized the success the adventure had yielded. By then, at the young age of 18, Nathan had developed some amazing skills as both a musician and audio engineer, and I had given him the responsibility of coproducing and fully engineering the recording of one of our music projects. It was a significant mental mountain to climb for such a young man. Add to that the unfortunate fact that some of our machines were breaking down during the process, leaving us stranded and scrambling to do repairs. Disasters such as these happened while high-dollar studio musicians were sitting idly, waiting for the sessions to re-start. It was, to say the least, a frustrating and costly journey toward completing the album.

Nathan was as weary as I was, but I'll never forget the moment when, during the playback of a final mix of one of the ten songs, he reached up and pushed the stop button on the recorder. He then looked over at me, and said, "Dad, I think I see the big blue bridge."

It was then that I knew our seven days together on bicycles had yielded a lesson he could use for a lifetime. Needless to say, I was so glad that I had not left him behind when I pedaled out of the Nashville area toward West Virginia three years before.

Daughters Like to Be with Daddy Too!

When Heidi came along, I was honestly a little nervous about whether or not a girl would like the outdoor stuff I liked to do. Still, I chose not to exclude my daughter. Heidi didn't take to hunting, but I discovered that we shared a love for fishing. We've spent many days together in pursuit of the larger fish that can be found in the big waters off the beaches of both sides of the Florida peninsula. One of the several trips we made to the deep portions of the Gulf of Mexico below Gulfport, Mississippi, yielded a memory that time will not likely erase.

We were innocently fishing below an oil rig about 45 miles off the banks of Gulfport when someone on the structure decided to dump their sewer system contents into our friend's newly restored boat. We had to tiptoe through the turnips. The disgustingly pungent load came down like a sudden rain. The terrible news is that we were without umbrellas.

Heidi got a direct hit of the "used manna." The tight, long curls of her hair contained the chunky evidence that someone didn't want us fishing around the rig. I quickly offered her a return to Gulfport, even though our day of fishing would abruptly end. It was in that moment that my 17-year-old girl revealed her unwavering love for angling in the big waters. She turned to me, and while pulling post-digested matter from her hair, she said, "Hey! It's only crap. Let's fish."

Her word choice caught me and our friend, Randy, totally off guard. But honestly, I was impressed. I was also grateful to learn just how much she enjoyed the sport of fishing.

Since that aromatic adventure, we have fished in places like the remote outer banks of Vancouver Island in Canada. Add to that our bicycle journey on the long-and-winding Natchez Trace Parkway that runs through Tennessee, Alabama, and Mississippi, as well as the numerous times we have canoed and kayaked down a favorite river near our home.

We have also traversed many miles of the Appalachian Trail together as a duo and with her brother, Nathan.

Though I love to recount these stories, this book is not about fatherhood. Do you remember my challenge about finding the two "hidden treasures" I found while including my kids in my hobbies? Did you note them? I have a feeling you already know what they are. But just to be clear, I will point out the pair of priceless pearls.

Forever Friends

One immeasurably valuable treasure that can be found in letting the kids tag along has been the closeness between us that was strengthened as a result of their involvement in my hobbies. Someone once said about kids growing up and departing the nest, "They leave as children, but they return as friends." Thankfully, this has been true for me and my two. Nathan and Heidi feel as much like my best of friends as they do my children. Though they have married wonderful spouses and have their own lives now, I cherish the times I see them come through the door for a visit. I do not regret the sacrifices that were required to accomplish the bond we enjoy.

Annie's Smile

The second treasure I enjoyed was that subtle smile that would be on Annie's face when I returned from an adventure with our kids. Very often I could tell that her expression was not just saying she was happy to see us safely home again or that she was pleased that her children enjoyed some bonding time with their father. It was also telling me, "Thanks for leaving me at home alone. I sure needed the break."

Whether I had taken the children to a local park for a couple of hours when they were very little or to the remote trails of the Great Smoky Mountain National Forest for a weekend when they were teens, Annie invariably would be revitalized by having some quiet downtime. This was for her a real gem. To put it humbly, including the kids in my passion for the outdoors as they were growing up was one thing I did right to help my wife not resent my love for the outdoors.

Dads, if you include your kids in your hobby, you too will see that same smile from time to time on your wife's face.

As a P.S. to this chapter about kids, you might wonder sometimes if they really do notice or appreciate the sacrifices related to your hobby that you make for them. Maybe this true story about a Pennsylvania hunter and his sons will encourage you to continue in your willingness to put them first.

The Hunter and His Gun

They were two old friends
Out on a November morning
Before the sun came over
That Pennsylvania mountain.
They slipped through the dark woods
Where the whitetail lives,
The hunter and his favorite old gun.

With his hard workin' hands
He tenderly nestled
The wood and the steel of
That .32 Special

'Cause he knew well
It would be the final season
For the hunter and his old gun.

'Cause he was thinkin' about
Three little boys
And how sad their faces would be
If Christmas came around
And there would be nothin'
Waitin' under the tree.
His pockets were empty;
It had been a lean year,
And he knew what had to be done.
It was a quiet farewell
On that November morning
For the hunter and his old gun.

Well he took what he got
For that old .32
And bought three toys
And three good pairs of shoes.
And three little smiles
Made Christmas that year
For the hunter and his sons.

He never mentioned
That old gun again,
But he could feel it in his arms
Now and then.
He just cradled the memory
Bitter and sweet
For the hunter and his gun.

But he was thinkin' about
Three little boys
And how sad their faces would be
If Christmas came around

And there would be nothin'
Waitin' under the tree.
His pockets were empty;
It had been a lean year,
But he did what had to be done.
It was a quiet farewell
On that November morning
For the hunter and his old gun.

And now in the heart
Of three grown-up boys
Is an ocean of thanks
'Cause they know the story
About a hard workin' daddy
And his sacrifice
He made for his loved ones.

So they tracked down that Winchester;
Dipped into their coffers.
They made a call
And made a real good offer.
They did it all just for the love
Between a hunter and his old gun.

'Cause they were thinkin' about
One fine man
And how happy his heart would be
If next season rolled around
And he was with his old friend
Under that big oak tree.
Their pockets were lighter
But it was worth it
They just did what their daddy would have done
And what a sweet reunion
'Tween two old friends
The hunter and his old gun.[3]

5

Your Leisure / Her Labor

nnie gave birth to both of our children using a pain-
management technique that was very popular in the early
1970s. It's known as the Lamaze method of childbirth. For
those who are not familiar with it, basically, in the moment when
an excruciating contraction would start, the husband stands behind
the mother-to-be and assists her as she begins a rapid, heavy
breathing, all the while keeping her eyes on a focal point to aid
in concentration. The combination of focusing and quick breathing
is meant to serve as a diversion from the pain, with the ultimate
goal being to benefit the infant with a natural, non-drug-induced
birthing. I can personally report that Lamaze works because when
each of our kids were born, *I didn't feel a thing!*

In order to learn how to achieve a successful organic childbirth,
it was necessary for us to go to a series of classes. I can still see
Annie and me sitting on the carpeted floor in a circle with five
other young couples. What a sight it was! There were six women

swelled to the point of bursting, and six men who were heavier than normal as a result of "eating for three" for nearly nine months. In total, we were 12 bloated human beings voluntarily hyper-ventilating as a group.

During the classes I managed to learn a great deal about some of the subtle nuances of a woman in pregnancy—things that would serve as useful signs that would guide me as I tried to understand and help Annie through the delivery. One of the most frightening was a particular warning each husband got from the course instructor. She said that during the latter stage of the birth process known as "transition," we could expect our wives to look at us angrily as they writhed in agonizing labor pains and dare us to ever come near them again. If a man wants to know fear, that's a place he can go to experience it. I've been there. It's really disturbing.

In the context of this "handbook for husbands with hobbies," there is one other very interesting thing I need to include that I learned about a woman during our Lamaze class. Every husband, young and old, should add this insight to his list of things to remember when it comes to helping his wife not hate what he loves to do.

I learned that Annie would, at some point prior to the birthing, suddenly experience what the teacher called "the nesting urge." It would be evidenced by a sudden, mysterious, and uncommonly strong zeal for doing things like sweeping, cleaning, cooking, and other types of activities necessary for housekeeping. (I was hoping that roofing the house and cutting a cord of firewood would be on the list of signs…but sadly, they weren't.) We were coached as husbands to watch for an escalation in her attention to these domestic details and, if we detected it, very likely the day of birthing could be very close. I did see it happen with Annie. And sure enough, our firstborn was delivered just a few days later.

—

But here's the deal. I thought the nesting urge Annie revealed just prior to our first delivery would subside after the birthday of our son. Not so. As best as I can tell, it has never really gone away. Because it seems to have remained in my wife, and it has appeared to have grown even more pronounced through the years, it makes me wonder if the attention she gives to caring for the shelter where we dwell is actually a "wiring issue" between our Creator and womankind. I have a feeling that the nesting urge was there all along, but the thing that turned that switch to the "on" position was our first pregnancy. Whatever the case, it seems to be a divine design.

The trouble is that some guys just don't see that trait in their wives. We can easily detect it in, for example, the bird world. Many of us have seen or even held the lightweight, bowl-shaped, empty remains of a robin's nest and been awed by the amount of work that must have been required to build and maintain such an intricate weaving of straw. Along with the birds, we have seen the nature documentaries on TV about other creatures such as alligators and rabbits busily readying homes for their families. While this is obvious in the animal world, some of us human males have never noticed that somewhere in the psyche of our wives is a similar urge.

For the men who have noted that their wives challenge them from time to time about how their hobby affects "the nest," and you have actually wondered why she does, this chapter is for you. For the remainder of guys who haven't caught on to this apparent mystery, I hope the next few pages will gently rattle your cage. And for all of my fellow sports fans, I hope to assist in helping you discover one of the most important things we can do to help our "nest mates" feel better about the obsessions we enjoy doing.

Help Needed!

Annie tells me that as satisfying as it can be for a woman to successfully maintain a clean presentable home, she admits that there is only one word that describes the process: work. To call it anything else would be an attempt to mask reality.

Not many ladies enjoy a "nasty nest," and in order to avoid it requires a nearly nonstop effort. Because so much physical energy is needed to accomplish such a task, Annie further informed me that perhaps the loudest and most consistent cry some women want to make as caregivers in the home is…"I can't do it by myself!"

How many of us as husbands have seen the faces of our sweet wives suddenly turn blood red, heard their teeth grind with rage, and then watched them pull at their disheveled hair, as they scream, "I need some help around here!" I would dare not use the word "demonic" to describe a wife's appearance in that moment, but *angelic* doesn't work either. What brought her to such an outburst? Unfortunately, there are times when the responsibility lies at the feet of her mate.

The one idea that follows is basically a behavioral guideline for husbands that can either help you maintain or help you restore tranquility in your nest. Your wife will be blessed if you follow through with this suggestion. You will sense a deeper level of calm in your home. Furthermore, your children might never be scared spitless again by their mother's occasional frightening change in personality.

A Cardinal Rule

The basic rule that I urge every husband to follow is: *Never let your play become her work.*

To explain what I mean by this friendly piece of advice, I have a personal story that will do the trick. A few years ago on a springtime day, I dropped Annie off at the airport around six o'clock in the evening so she could fly out to fulfill a speaking engagement the next morning. I was to pick her up the following evening. It was one of the rare times that I could stay behind and get some things done that needed to be taken care of around the house. The next morning I awoke very early and did what I usually do when a lot of work needs to be done. I went fishing.

The crappie were biting big time that morning, and by ten o'clock I was back home with a full stringer. I cleaned the fish at the kitchen sink, and then stored the tasty fillets in the freezer for a future feeding. While in the garage at the freezer, I remembered that one of the jobs I wanted to get done was to straighten up that area. I closed the freezer door and went right to work.

As is often the case when I begin a task, I fully intend to focus on that one thing without wavering. However, if I see something that reminds me of another task I want to complete, I have a personality flaw that makes me prone to start another chore before finishing the former job. In other words, when it comes to doing household repairs and maintenance, I have been known to use the "rabbit trail" method. Also, while jumping from one thing to the next, I can easily lose track of time, space, and even forget to eat. That's what happened to me that morning.

Needless to say, the hour to head to the airport came quickly. Without cleaning up at all, I locked the back door, jumped into the car, and headed to town to meet my dearly beloved. When she climbed into the car she commented about how my appearance made it obvious to her that a lot of work had probably been done at the house. She was excited. However, when we got home and entered as we always do—through the back door—her delight suddenly turned to despair. My nose told me why.

As we stood in the kitchen holding our breath, I mentally (and quickly) retraced my steps through the day. I realized that after I closed the door of the freezer around 11 and went straight to work in the garage, I failed to go back to the sink in the kitchen to clean up the fish remains. I didn't go back into the house all day even for a drink because the refrigerator that stood next to the freezer in the garage was full of bottles of cold drinks. And because I forget to eat, I had no cause to go back to the kitchen. Furthermore, everything I needed to do was outside. Man…I was in a heap of serious trouble.

Almost in tears, Annie walked over to the sink and looked at what appeared to be a murder sight. The dried blood and guts that were piled in the porcelain sink was the source of the foul stench that permeated our residence. Big drops of sweat began to form on the back of my legs, and I was speechless as I stood there…guilty of temporary insanity in the first degree.

How on earth could I have possibly forgotten such a detail? The answer is easy…'cause I can be a complete idiot sometimes, that's why. The signs that revealed that I had stolen some of the morning to go to the lake and kill some fish were really hard to hide. But thieving "honey do" time was not the crime. Annie would likely have been perfectly fine with my enjoyment of some leisure. The felony was in our poor kitchen, our living room, our bedrooms, as well as in places like the fabric of our couch, our curtains, pillows, and tablecloths. And Annie was afraid it might even be in our wall paper!

Offering no defense for my heinous act, I started toward the sink to remove the disgusting remains. Before I could say "go ahead and shoot me," Annie had grabbed a plastic spatula and a handful of paper towels and started scraping the ugly death off the sides of the tubs. Having been duly informed that I was incapable of knowing what all had to be done to purge our home from such an unwelcome aroma, Annie sent me outside to finish following the domestic rabbit trail I had been on.

I begged to help her but to no avail. It took days before our house smelled normal again. At least that's what we assumed. We feared for the longest time that we had gotten so used to the odor that we simply couldn't detect it. In fact, several times we went outside for a few minutes and breathed fresh air for a while, and then we'd go back in to see if our noses were telling us the truth. Finally, after a great deal of effort on Annie's part, she was satisfied that the damage I had rendered to the environment in our home had been fixed.

I had violated one of the cardinal rules for husbands, and because we men forget so easily, it bears repeating: *Never let your play become her work.*

I have heard from many wives who have dealt with sportsmen like me who can be smart one minute and numbskulls the next. Here are a few other reports of those who have broken this particular "red" rule. I do not include these comments for the purpose of contributing to a feeling of camaraderie between those of us who have made the same unforgettable blunders, but to warn us all that if we continue to do these kinds of things, our house is going to stink with unhappiness!

> The Good Husband's Principle
>
> **Never let your play become her work**

❑ *When my husband gets up before daylight to go deer hunting, he usually dresses under the patio. However, I can always tell when he forgot something and had to come back inside before driving away. The linoleum in the kitchen has a trail of little squiggley clumps of dried mud from the back door to wherever he went inside. The shape of the squigglies match the tread pattern on the bottom of his boots exactly. I can't tell you how many mornings I have gotten up and the first thing I had to do was sweep the floor that was perfectly clean the night before. I beg him to not do it, but I think there are clumps of mud in his ears.*

This may seem like an insignificant complaint to some but

there's more to this statement than mud squigglies. By repeating this mistake, this guy is saying to his wife, "I really don't care how you feel." Preventing this mistake is not only necessary, thankfully it is extremely easy. When I deer hunt, I often wear tall, lace-up boots. I know what a hassle it can be to get them on and off. However, the trick I've learned is to wear a pair of low-cut shoes on the way to where I'm going to hunt and put the boots on after I get there. Not only will this eliminate the mud-trail error in the house, it says volumes of sweet things to a wife. Besides that, there is an advantage in regard to the hunt. Not putting your boots on and wearing them through your house reduces the risk of picking up odors on your boots (wax, cleanser). It's just one more thing you can do to outsmart the very sensitive olfactory system of the wily whitetail.

❏ *My husband butchers his own deer at home and throws the carcass over the fence in the backyard for the dogs. The bad news is that our dogs chew on the bones and many times break them up and drag them into our main yard and onto our unpaved driveway. While it's bad enough that our front yard looks like a burial ground excavation site, there is a worse problem. At the most inopportune times, I have gotten into my car to go somewhere and, while maneuvering to leave, I have run over one of the broken, sharp-edged bone remnants sticking up out of the ground. A tire gets punctured. Next thing I know I'm either trying to change the tire or calling someone for help...because my husband is either at work or out hunting!*

Every hunter knows that when the trigger is pulled or the arrow flies, the fun ends and work begins. Having dragged many a deer out of the woods and skinned them at home, I know how tired a fellow can be toward the end of the process. That's when it's tempting to take the least line of resistance and let nature finish the cleanup. That's not smart.

The messy hunter is creating two problems for his wife. One is the emotional labor of embarrassment that comes with feeling like the outside appearance of their house is that of the Addams Family. The other is the frustrating effort it takes to deal with schedule delays caused by deer bone fragments in tires.

First of all, this fellow is obviously blind to the fact that his front yard might cause visitors to question the character of the residents of the house. Second, you'd think the money that a fellow would be shelling out for new tires would get his attention. Apparently not!

To resolve his twofold problem, there's only one thing this husband can do: He should get rid of the dogs...yeah, right! Just kidding. Since that is not likely to happen, there's another way. If he's going to keep the dogs and treat them to leftover venison, then he could build a pen that will serve as both a critter cafeteria (to confine the dogs during their free lunch) and a bone collection center. When the bones are picked clean, he can carry them to the dump or somewhere else that would prevent the dogs from doing their bad deeds. If the hunter refuses to help his wife out in this way, tires are not all that are going to go flat.

❏ *Bird hunting with dogs is my husband's passion. Along with that, he loves to breed and raise prize retrievers. I love the dogs, too, but not as housemates. The carnage that our big dogs can render to the interior of our house is unbelievable. I am constantly vacuuming hair and shampooing carpets.*

I love dogs, too. We had a Shitzu named Bob. He has gone to the place all good dogs go when they die, but when he was living his favorite place to sleep was on our couch. The bad news is that in his later years, Bob could smell like a combination of wet chicken and soured, infected ear wax. As much as Annie appreciated my affection for Bob, she basically tolerated his presence. She didn't think a dog was meant to be inside…especially parked on our nice couch.

I ended up cutting large pieces of cardboard to use as blocking walls to keep Bob out of the den while we were not at home. And while we were there, I took it upon myself to make sure Bob would not jump up on the couch. If he wanted to sit on it, he had to sit on my lap.

Obviously, there are many ways to remedy the inside dog messes. The real question is, Will a fellow be smart enough to do it? He will…unless he enjoys being in the doghouse.

❑ *One year at Christmas my husband opened a gift I got for him. When he looked at the very nice wool sweater, he said, "I promise not to get blood on it!" There was a reason he made that statement. Many times he gets deer or turkey blood on his good clothes, leaving the job to me to remove it. He thinks I have some sort of magic power to erase the stains.*

I'm guilty by association. Annie has dealt with this legitimate complaint more times than I want to admit. The solution, once again, is simple. Don't accept presents of wool clothing or any other "nice" garment that would feel good on a cold day in the deer-stand.

Seriously, getting out of the good duds only takes a few extra minutes. But every hunter knows it's not always convenient to completely redress ourselves when its 3:30 in the afternoon in late October and you've gone straight from work to a nearby farm to hunt. Sunset is only an hour-and-a-half away, and you want to be in the treestand or at a field edge as quickly as you can. To do so, slipping the camo coveralls over the dress clothes is a matter of expedience. A little scent suppression spray, and you're on your way into the woods. But then it happens.

Bang! (or if you're bowhunting...*Thwap!*) Now you've got a deer down. Finding and field dressing it is foremost on your mind...not your wardrobe. That, my fellow hunter, is how we can get into the blood-on-the-good-clothes transgression. Surely, for the sake of the marriage, we can do better.

> ❑ *I'm not sure if this qualifies for your question about conflicts related to any extra work involved with my husband's interest, but I have to constantly "work" through something in regard to his love of hunting. As proud as I am of his accomplishments, I am yet to understand why our home has to be decorated with the taxidermied evidence of his exploits. I feel like our décor could be categorized somewhere between a zoo and a morgue. The worst part is, I feel like I have no say in the matter. When I even hint at wanting more elegance in terms of decorating, I get "the eye." I wish we could afford a separate room for all the mounts.*

Among the many comments about husband/wife/hobby conflicts that were given in response to my inquiry, one of the subjects frequently mentioned was taxidermy. As was the case for this lady, most of the women didn't necessarily resent their husband's hunting, but it was his unwillingness to budge when it came to the wall mounts that bothered them most.

Without a doubt, the hunter mentioned sees the house he lives in as *his* and not *theirs*. If this poor woman gets the cold shoulder whenever she even suggests a décor change, there's only one word to describe his stance...self-centered.

My fellow hobbyists, please don't think me weak or wimpy when I tell you this, but I have yielded to my wife's wishes when it comes to home décor. With her permission, I have three mounts on the walls in our home. In my little office you will find a South Dakota mule deer head sporting a 5 x 5 set of antlers, our son's first Tennessee six-point buck, and in our laundry room there is an Arizona javelina head. The javelina is mounted with a vicious look and wears a Dale Earnhardt baseball cap. We affectionately call him our "laundry guardian."

That's all I'm allowed, and I willingly submit to the limitations. Why? Because Annie is the one who feels the nesting urge! I learned that lesson in 1977…remember? Since that Lamaze educational achievement, life as a married man and a hunter has been sweet on the home decoration front. But recently, at the time of this writing, a challenge has come to the two of us. It involves a bear rug.

Remember earlier in the chapter about giving her equal time I jokingly said that I had gone to Montana to eliminate a black bear that I was sure would migrate to Annie's garden and eat up all her flowers? Well, I really did it. A nice 300-pound, coal-black bear crossed my path, and I harvested him. As I type I await the rug that is being made out of the pelt.

I'm not sure why I succumbed to ordering a bear rug but I did. I knew very well when I agreed to it that I would not have a place to lay it or hang it. Yet I made the monetary deposit, and about 12 months from the kill date I should receive my prize.

I was surprised that the process takes about a year to complete. But I think I know why it takes so long. There is a tactical reason for it. In reality, I think it takes the taxidermist only a week or so to complete the job. He just knows better than to send it out right away. He knows that if he did ship his furry art out immediately, most of the rugs would come back to him undelivered. Why? I can personally report that it probably takes about a year for a wife to adjust to the news that her home is going to be getting a bear rug!

The questionnaire responses included in this chapter were limited to ladies whose husbands are hunters, golfers, and dog owners. There are, of course, many other sportsmen whose hobbies have become the source of their wives' extra work. All of us, no matter what we enjoy doing, would be wise to take a careful look at how our interests affect our spouse. Remember this: When it comes to what we enjoy doing as a pastime, the trophy of all trophies is her hardy approval of it. If you can hang that on the wall of your hearts, you'll really have something to be proud of!

6

Your Fun / Her Fear

There may be a very good reason that no one knows what another day may bring. If humans had that kind of knowledge, I have a feeling the streets would not bustle like they do, airports would be empty, the highways would be vacant, and deer hunters would never get up in trees.

If I would have awakened on that August day a few years ago knowing that by midday I would be descending rapidly toward earth in a free fall, I would have turned over and gone back to sleep. Instead, I casually entered the woods wearing shorts and a T-shirt and carrying the equipment I needed to hang an old treestand permanently in the forks of a tall red oak.

As I stood on the wooden platform about 18 feet above the hard, late-summer ground, I was nearing the completion of my plan. All I had to do was make one more little adjustment, and the green-painted plywood floor would find its final resting place in the spot I had picked out for it just a day or two before.

Suddenly, I was suspended in air...but only for a microsecond. The only thing holding the dangling square piece of wood to my feet were the two heavy-duty cloth straps that were around the toes of my tennis shoes. Both the stand and I plunged toward the planet.

I have no one else to thank except Almighty God for what happened in the next moment. I'll never know why, but it occurred to me that I should reach out and wrap my arms around the tree. So I did. The thing I didn't think about was how rough the bark was. As I plummeted toward what I assumed would be a deadly sudden stop, I hardly felt the tree bark scraping against my fingers and arms. It all took place so quickly.

I didn't splatter on the ground like I expected. Instead, the forks of the tree came together about four feet off the ground. The treestand got to that point and slammed to a stop. I was forced to let go of the trunk. I folded over backward in the shape of the letter "C." One foot broke the strap of the stand. The other foot was caught in the second strap, and it held me to the platform as I dangled one-legged and upside down, still bent over backward.

I must have wiggled my foot just a little because suddenly I was set free to drop to the ground. I realized that I was still alive and was very happy to know that I could move. Slowly I maneuvered my body to a seated position and sat there assessing the feelings I was having.

Nothing seemed to be seriously damaged, so I put one hand on the ground and with the other I leaned against the tree to help myself stand upright. The happiness I felt in knowing I could walk was immense. I waited for shooting pains. Nothing hurt at the moment...nothing but my fingers.

I held my hands out in front of me to see why they were stinging and gasped at the sight of the shredded flesh. The fingers that got the worst damage were on my left hand—the very appendages that press on guitar strings and make chords by which my wife and I sing…for a living! I later realized that my left hand took most of the abuse because the fork of the tree I was working on leaned to the right, making my left hand the primary connection as I descended.

My other hand was about half as chewed up. As I studied that hand, my inner arms started stinging. Salty sweat poured into the bloody, exposed flesh that was scraped unmercifully by the rugged bark of the tree. My left arm was much worse than the right. Then my inner thighs began to announce that they had not been spared from the carnage.

The stinging intensified in my hands, and the only thing that offered any relief was to gently swing my arms. At the moment I thought it might have helped to dance a little with the pain, but for fear of finalizing some yet unknown injury, I just went in circles with small deliberate steps, sort of like a chicken. I was grateful I could actually walk.

I could have died that day. I'm not being melodramatic. Some have done just that as a result of treestand accidents. Others are paralyzed. I was mortified by what could have been. In my state of conscious shock, I knew I had to get home and clean the open wounds. I left the stand lodged where it came to rest in the lower fork of the tree, gathered my few tools, and headed to the truck. It was a ten-minute walk to my pickup. On the way I fought the burning sting of more summer salty sweat that ran like fire across my raw flesh. I also tried not to think of how bad the alcohol wash was going to feel when I poured it onto the wounds. However, there was a dread that was worse. I had to face Annie when I got home.

Why was I so apprehensive about letting Annie see and hear about what had happened? Very simply, there's a rule that every husband with a potentially dangerous hobby should try to live by.

That day, though it was not intentional, I had broken that rule. It is: *Don't let your fun become her fear.*

I was nervous about her seeing my bloody arms, fingers, and legs. I dreaded her knowing that I had no idea what else might have been hurt but would show up later. What would she say? How would she feel? And, most important, would I ever be able to win back her confidence that I am a safe hunter? These questions stung my heart.

When I got home, Annie was gone. *Whew!* I hurried to the bathroom and began the self-treatment. That was not fun, to say the least, but finally I applied anti-bacterial salve on all the wounds, wrapped my forearms with dressings, and put Band-Aids on all my injured fingers. I put on some clean jeans, a long sleeve shirt, and waited for my appointment with the truth. Finally I heard the back door open.

Annie took one look at me and with obvious horror asked, "What on earth happened, Steve?"

"Oh, I had a little fall."

Obviously not buying the "little" part of my story, she further inquired, "And just where did this fall take place?"

Thus began my walk down Humble Lane. I really didn't want to reveal the scary details of what had happened, but I figured she would eventually know. I gave her all the details.

> **The Good Husband's Principle**
>
> **Don't let your fun become her fear**

Since that day, no matter what I do, whenever I head to the woods to hunt deer, I know that the memory of my painful fall probably crosses her mind. In order to console her, I have doubled the guarantee regarding safety measures. For example, I have added a cell phone to my camo pants pocket with a promise to connect if I'm going to be late. I write her notes if I leave before daylight, just to make sure she knows where I'll be and when I'll get back. Plus, I don't go to the woods alone as much as I used to.

Many men have other hobbies that have inherent dangers, such as motorcycling, bicycling, four-wheeling, snowmobiling, speed boating, mountain climbing, hockey, scuba diving, sky diving... do I need to keep going? Basically, if you leave the house to do anything out of sight of your wife, to some degree or another you run the risk of tampering with her sense of comfort. For that reason I urge you to consider how she feels about it and do all that you can to put her at ease.

I've mentioned a few things that I do to help Annie not be so fearful when I go hunting. On the list of other things men do that have an element of danger involved, the following suggestions will help your wife not hate your hobby. These ideas come from a question asked to ladies that addressed their spouses' inherently dangerous interests: *What is the number one thing that you wish your husband would do to help you not worry about him while he is engaged in his hobby?*

❑ *Check in as often as possible.*

Coming from the wife of a man who developed an interest in long-range bicycling at the ripe young age of 49, this is not an unreasonable request. Because she cares enough about him to want to know he's unharmed, investing in a cell phone is the obvious solution for him. If one cannot be obtained, this fellow should stop and call from a hard line reasonably often. The sound of his voice could make all the difference between his wife having calm or chaos in her heart while he's away. The truth is, a working cell phone is a very smart item for anyone to have while doing activities that have health risks.

❑ *Make sure your equipment is in tip-top shape.*

This wish came from the wife of a fan of rapelling and rock climbing. Assuring his wife of the excellent working condition of his equipment is a must. Along with that, she should be confident that he is well-skilled in handling it. Other types of hobby-supporting items, such as guns, bows, mountain bikes, motorized vehicles, and parachutes, are not just toys to some women. If your wife thinks you may be unfamiliar with the machinery, unskilled, or unable to be level-headed while using your gear, then these items, in her mind, become implements of destruction.

To ignore that your wife might feel this way overlooks the valuable intuition of the female that could very well spare you from future harm. I can personally attest to this potential. As an avid lover of long-distance running, I set a goal for myself to run a full marathon when I turned 40. I trained relentlessly, sometimes running ten miles a day. For some strange reason, Annie kept mentioning her concern for my knees. She would say, "Those knees were meant for a lifetime!" I should have listened to her.

In 1990, I did indeed run the marathon I had dreamed of completing. That was in December. In March of 1991, I had to have knee surgery. I had worn out the inside of my right knee cap. Today, I humbly admit that I would have been wise to have seriously considered Annie's intuition.

❏ *My husband loves his motorcycle. I have some reservations about him being on the highway so unprotected, but I'm not going to stop him. My only wish is that he would at least wear his helmet.*

This wife is not asking for much at all. Raising her comfort level would be a very doable thing. Besides, if her happiness is his chief concern, her wish should be his command. I have a motorcycle also, as well as a wife who views it with her fingernails between her teeth. She has asked me to do two things when it comes to riding. One, don't ride in the rain, at least not intentionally. Two, stay off the Interstate highways. The second request is born out of some sights we have seen on our super highways.

Sometimes when we're in our car and she sees a bike pass us rolling along at about 80 or 90 miles per hour and weaving in and out of traffic, Annie has been known to say one or two or sometimes both of the following phrases: "Pin head!" or the well-known "Donor biker!"

Neither choice of words is meant as a character assessment of the passing rider. At least, that's what I assume. Instead, I hear it as a hint to me that says, "Please don't be so small-minded and careless." She has often mentioned that the total absence of protection a biker has other than his "brain bucket" (her preferred description of a helmet) makes absolutely no sense to her. I have learned to take note of these remarks and never ride without caution.

❑ *I don't fear for my husband's health as much as I do for the damage some of his friends might do to his morals.*

A very real fear that some women express is an apprehension regarding the friends that their husbands keep in relationship to their hobbies. There's an old adage that someone recently twisted just a bit. His rewrite says, "Give a man a fish, and you'll feed him for a day. Teach a man to fish, and he'll sit in a boat all day and drink beer with his friends."

Unfortunately, some wives would totally agree. A wife may see her husband's questionable friendships as a threat to her mate's integrity. What can result is a gnawing fear for her husband's moral well-being. Believing that "bad company corrupts good morals," she may challenge his choice of companions, giving rise to a very serious conflict. If this issue has ever come up between you and your wife, I strongly encourage you to take it seriously, even if it means discreetly cutting the ties with those who do not generate the good favor of your wife.

No matter how hard we try to keep our wives' apprehensions to a minimum, accidents do happen. But what is at issue here is not that accidents can happen. The real deal is, Can she trust you to do all you can to avoid them? If you can give her that assurance, it is much more likely that your fun will not become her fear.

7

Don't Mess with Traditions

The question little starving children sometimes ask: "What time is Christmas dinner?"

The answer that mothers and grandmothers often give: "We can't eat until the men get back from hunting."

I have a feeling this exchange has caused more blood pressures to rise through the years than nearly any other conversation during the holidays. How many times have mud-caked fathers and sons, brothers and in-laws stepped into a house at a moment when the fuming anger over their lateness for the customary family holiday meal has reached a festivity-destroying crescendo? Appetites wane as word bullets zing across beautifully decorated dining rooms. Children run in horror, but apron-clad mothers grab them just before they disappear and dare them to delay the feast another minute. This disastrous scene has been repeated far too many times. The hunters have once again messed with a tradition.

This chapter will not be long. I want to leave you plenty of time to get to the dinner table lest you be guilty of this mistake and be exiled to your room without nourishment. Suffice it to say that if you want to sow the seeds of your wife's resentment for your hobby, then all you have to do is consistently violate the unspoken rule that comes into play around holidays. That rule is: *This is our time, not your time.*

Traditional holiday mealtimes are not the only candidates for the list of scheduled things a smart sportsman will be careful not to tamper with. Here are a few others:

Weekly church functions	Funerals
Birthday parties	Dinner parties with *reservations*
Anniversaries	Family reunions
Graduations	Easter events
Retirement parties	Thanksgiving dinner
Ball games	Date nights with spouse
School performances	Vacation trip plane departures
Weddings	Valentine getaways
Birthings!	

If you added the scheduled events and activities that I haven't thought of, the list could be unending. While it is likely that every husband has his own unique commitment to keep, there may be one or two (or more) on the list above that ring your bell. And on the day or in the hour that it does ring, when (not if) you hear it, don't ignore it. A lot of guys have made that mistake, which reminds me of a story that's been floating around for years about a golfer who missed an important event.

It seems a group of seasoned citizen hackers were standing on a green that happened to be next to a highway. A funeral procession came by and one of the fellows removed his cap, put it over his heart, and held it there until the long line of cars finally passed. Impressed with his friend's display of courtesy, one of the other guys said, "Man, you are to be commended for showing such respect to the dead."

The solemn golfer put his hat back on, addressed his putt, and replied, "She was a good wife for over 40 years."

I've never stooped to those depths when it comes to messing with traditions, but I did nearly make just as deadly a mistake a few years ago. Not only did I almost go astray, I came real close to inviting my hunting-buddy son and my rookie hunter son-in-law-to-be to go with me down the deadly path of messing with a sacred event.

For some strange reason, yet to be understood by this deer hunter, my daughter and her groom decided their wedding day would be November 25. Does that date trigger anything in your mind? If you love to pursue the whitetail deer in the territory where we live, you'll know immediately that the first day of gun season usually starts around Thanksgiving. That year the opening day fell on, you guessed it…November 25.

I rehearsed it every possible way I could, but when it came out of my mouth, it fell to the ground like a ball of ugly lead. What did I say? "Annie, you know the first day of deer season is Saturday (the wedding day). I think Nathan and Emmitt and I could be out of the woods and back to the church on time to get our tuxes on and all that other stuff if we went out hunting for just a couple of hours. What do you think?"

The slight snarl that suddenly appeared on Annie's upper lip resembled that of Elvis'. However, the song she wanted to sing was not a love song. With a quietly stern voice that only a loving wife could use to get a clear message across to her insane husband, she said, "If you go hunting Saturday morning, you'll never get out of the woods!"

Did we go? On the morning of Saturday, November 25, I can tell you where I *wasn't*. I was not sitting peacefully in a tree at daylight. I was not pulling a trigger, and I was not following a blood trail. Where was I? Doing what any smart man would do who had been given an ultimatum regarding the future quality of his marriage. I was eating breakfast with the wedding party, showering, trimming my beard, and polishing my black shoes. Was I on time for the ceremony? You bet. And I am glad I was. So was Emmitt and one of his main groomsmen, Nathan.

It's hard to believe that some men would actually trade one more hour of hunting, fishing, biking, softball, or any other thing over the good will of his wife. But as crazy as it sounds, we can all be guilty of this transgression. Guys, I encourage us all to remember that, if our wives expect us to be on time for family traditions and special events, they are likely not doing so in an attempt to "hen peck" us. Rather, they are concerned about our mental and emotional health. Very simply, they know that if we continue to intentionally ignore their feelings, we will suffer. And who wants that? Now, hurry up and be on time!

8

From Passion to Mission

S ince the mid-1970s, my wife and I have traveled as musicians to hundreds of cities and towns across our great nation. As a result, I have had the opportunity to meet a lot of fellows from all walks of life. As I talk with men, one particular subject reoccurs. Many of them seem to live with an unmet longing in their hearts to do something they consider as "meaningful" to others. While none of them regret their role as providers for their families, some have candidly admitted that in terms of impacting the world beyond their doorsteps, their jobs seem mundane and unimportant. Some have even tearfully expressed their deep yearning for a feeling of significance.

My soul aches for those who may feel that their lives are not fulfilling. I wrote the following lyric with hopes that I could help some of these men realize that the work they do on an everyday basis accomplishes a very vital and eternal purpose, one that they may not even know they have.

The Master's Plan

One made the wood,
One made the nails.
Another swung the hammer
And one made the sails.
Lotta hard work
For the men to do
So a ship could sail
On the waters blue.

But they didn't know
How the work of their hands
Was gonna fit in
To the Master's plan.
They might have thought
It was just a job,
But it was so much more,
In the hands of God.

'Cause without that ship,
How would we know
When the waves get high
And the hard winds blow
There's only one
Who can calm the stormy seas?
God speaks through the works of men—
Workin' men like you and me.

One made the plow,
One farmed the field
Somebody cut the stone,
For the grinding wheel
Somebody made an oven
For the baker to use
And somebody fished
The waters blue.

But they didn't know
How the work of their hands
Was gonna fit in
To the Master's plan
They might have thought
It was just a job,
But it was so much more
In the hands of God.

'Cause without that fish and bread
How would we know
When times get hard
And the money gets low,
The Lord can take a little
And make it all we need?
God speaks through the works of men—
Workin' men like you and me.

Maybe you don't know
How the work of your hands
Is gonna fit in
To the Master's plan.
You might think
It's just a job,
But it's so much more
In the hands of God.

Without that ship
How would we know
He can talk to the wind
And lay the waters down low?
The fish and bread reminds us
He can meet our needs.
God speaks through the works of men—
Workin' men like you and me.[4]

If you are among those who have ever wondered whether or not your life has meaning, I hope this lyric opened your eyes to a truth you may have never considered. It is incredible how God can network the labor of our hands to accomplish His grand purposes. That truly is good news for working men like you and me. But the news gets even better if you are a husband with a serious hobby!

Not only can your job hold the potential for affecting others in a positive way, but your hobby can accomplish that goal as well. And as a wonderful side benefit, your wife might see something in how you use your interest to impact other lives that could very well endear her to what you do in a way you would never expect.

For example, as you well understand by now, I am addicted to hunting. Deer, turkey, bear, elk, ducks, coyotes, roaches...if it moves I'm in pursuit of it. (And I want everyone to know that I eat all I harvest—except coyotes and roaches.) Annie is very aware of my obsession and would admit that at times I have been quite excessive in the doing of it. However, a significant difference in how she views what I love to do came as a result of an idea I came upon one day...while on a hunting trip.

I'll never forget the moment the notion came to me to write the book *A Look at Life from a Deer Stand*. My son and I were at Maranatha Bible Camp in central Nebraska for a bow-hunting event. The schedule for the hunt included a nightly time of sitting around the fireplace after the evening meal and sharing from our hearts with each other. The subjects of discussion ranged from stories of hunts gone by to dreams of hunts in the future, from tips that would improve our archery skills to hilarious blunders and even frightening close calls. Of all the types of comments that were offered, the ones that seemed to resurface each evening were the insights about life that the hunters had gleaned from the woods.

As I sat and took it all in, I realized that as a hunter I had some of the very same thoughts that the others encountered. One evening it suddenly occurred to me that it would be an interesting adventure to gather some of the spiritual, philosophical, and physically beneficial types of lessons I had "harvested" while hunting and compile them into a book. By the fall season of the next year, my personally imposed assignment had been completed.

As I mentioned in the introduction of this book, *A Look at Life from a Deer Stand* has connected with hundreds of thousands of other hunters. I think this happened because so much of the content of the writing touched a familiar place in the minds and hearts of readers. In addition, the book became a resource for wives who wanted to give something to their hunter-husbands as a gift that offered something more than a how-to on "blood-letting."

One wife, for example, came to me after an evening concert in Ohio. She handed me a dog-eared copy of the book and smiled as she said, "My husband is working and couldn't be here tonight, but he wanted me to bring this book for you to sign. I've been married to him for 23 years, and I've never seen him read one single book...until I got this one for him. I guess he's read it through three or four times. Thank you for taking the time to write it. He's a different man today." It was a humbling statement to say the least.

One other letter stands out in my mind and heart as confirmation that I had rightly responded to the idea to write the book. It came from a hunter who sent a photocopy of a note he had received from his dad. The note was written on the inside front cover of my first book that the father had read and then given to his son. It said:

> Mike,
>
> I hope you enjoy this book as much as I did. I can see now why you love deer hunting so much. I imagine you have had many deep thoughts as you waited in your treestand as this man did. I am thankful you have this to invest some of your time in. I pray that you send your "arrows" in the

right direction. I want to share some outdoor time with you and your arrows.

Love,

Dad

What more could I expect from such a simple thing as deciding to write a book about something I love to do? All I did was respond to a dream. The reality of it, to say the least, has been over- whelming. The personal benefits cannot be fully stated; however, the one outcome that pleases me as much as anything else is that Annie has been the first beneficiary of my choice to *turn a passion into a mission*.

The Good Husband's Principle

Turn your passion into your mission

I believe she is delighted that no longer is my purpose for hunting a matter of personal gratification. While she doesn't doubt that I still long for the raw adventure of the hunt, she knows that now I have higher goals for going "out there." I feel compelled to not only find food for our table, but also to look for the soul-feeding nourishment of the transforming truth avail- able in God's great outdoors. When I find it, I enjoy writing about it and making it available to other sportsmen. Sometimes I cap- ture the sights and sounds of a life-changing outdoor insight and create visual tools for teaching. As I create material for this pur- pose, Annie can see my appetite for making something useful out of my time spent in the woods. Seeing that hunger has become one more reason for her to appreciate what I like so much to do.

There are others I have met who have won the favor of their wives (and families) by turning their passions into missions. New York resident, award-winning photographer, celebrated author, and expert hunter Charles Alsheimer is a prime example of the value of "redeeming a passion." His love of understanding the whitetail deer in combination with his incredible photographic and writing talents have turned his life as a hunter into a huge educational resource for the deer hunting community. Along with that, Charlie remains one of the most sought-after speakers in America when it comes to hunting related events. While I have spoken at a few of the same places where Charlie has been previously featured, I'll admit without reservation that I am a little dubious about following in his steps. It's not easy to win the favor of an audience when they've already seen and heard the best.

Charlie's published expertise as a photographer can be found in book after book. One of the best samples of his work can be seen on the cover of *A Look at Life from a Deer Stand*. I'm convinced that Charlie's photo has done as much as anything else to help get the book into the hands of readers.

Perhaps greater than any other accomplishment, Charlie's love for his family that he reveals in his writing and photography has inspired hundreds of thousands of hunters to strive toward prioritizing their lives just as he has done.

His wife, Carla, writes,

> When we mutually decided 25 years ago that Charlie would leave the corporate world behind to pursue his dream, we did what many considered a radical thing at the time. To us it was a step of faith. Aaron was two years old when father and son set out on this journey. We did not want to put our youngster in daycare, so Charlie took on the role of a stay-at-home dad. Little did we realize at the beginning what a wonderful bond would develop between them over time. This has been a special blessing, not just to the two of them, but to me as well....
>
> In addition two other things come to mind as blessings we have experienced since Charlie turned his passion into a mission. First, he is happy doing what he does. He

has a genuine enthusiasm for life and for his life's work. Second is that he has met so many wonderful people. Our lives have been enriched with new friends from many different places. Occasionally a letter of thanks or affirmation arrives from someone whose life he has touched, and it gives us a renewed sense that the passion he has for sharing God's creation is well worth the energy he puts into it.

Charlie's son, Aaron, adds,

Most people know my dad as a gifted photographer and a skilled deer hunter. My unique vantage point has allowed me to see him as a man of deep faith and exceptional integrity. I can't imagine a father and son being closer than we are. He is my best friend and my most important role model. He has always made time for me, and because [of] his commitment to be a father first and an outdoor writer/photographer second, he has had a positive impact on virtually every aspect of my life. His values have become my values. Dad has encouraged me to chase my dreams, and he and mom have given selflessly in order to give me that opportunity.

While it would be difficult to number the whitetail hunters who have greatly benefited by Charlie Alsheimer's full-time commitment to his many skills, it is obvious that the two people who have gained the most from his choice to turn his passion into a mission are his wife and son.

Many of us, if we were honest, would dearly love to be able to do what Charlie does every day. In fact, a host of us would admit that we are just a bit envious of his position. (Go ahead...sigh deeply with me and say it..."It's a tough job, but somebody has to do it!") However, there are some shining examples of those who have managed to successfully use their passion as a mission even while maintaining a full-time job in the "9 to 5 world." The time devoted to using their hobby as a way to "make a difference" may be somewhat limited, yet they have made the effort and it has paid off.

One person in this category who comes to mind is a friend and fellow angler in the western state of Washington. His name is Jim Grenz. Jim's unusual love of fishing has gone way beyond a thirst for wetting his own line. Today his mission is to use his annual summer getaways from his occupation (he's a real-estate manager) as a tool to bless other fishermen. There is quite a long list of those who have been privileged to climb aboard Jim's boat and sail to places where only God and His awesome creation serve as the entertainment. Thankfully, my daughter and I are on it.

Jim took Heidi and me on a three-day fishing excursion off the coast of Canada. It was absolutely without exception three of the best days we ever spent in our lives. Heidi was to be married not many months after the trip. That sentimental element made our journey even more special because it would be the last father/daughter adventure we would have before she became Mrs. Emmitt Beall.

As he does for all his guests, Jim made sure that each morning following our arrival at the designated fishing spot we took a few minutes to thank the Creator who had made the place we were enjoying. He knew very well that our day would go better once the thanks that was due our heavenly Father was offered.

What does his wife think of what Jim does? Having been in the Grenz home and knowing his wife, Kay, I can tell you that she is extremely proud of her husband for turning what used to be an obsession into an activity that now has an eternal purpose.

Kay reports,

> Jim has had a passion for fishing for as long as I can remember. As time passed and he was able to spend more

time on the water, he got his first boat. It was a long and patient wait. He immediately began to wonder how he could use the boat to be a "fisher of men." Eventually, he began to invite both churched and unchurched men, and very often their kids, to accompany him to his favorite fishing waters. The outcome has been fantastic. One gentleman wrote Jim a letter after their trip, and said, "...the scenery was unsurpassed and the fishing was fabulous. But what I will remember the most is how you use your boat to show faith to others."

Kay continues, "I'm so proud of Jim and his desire to be available to others. People often ask me, 'How can you let him be gone for so long?' The answer is easy. He's a man on a mission to introduce others to a faith in Jesus Christ, and that makes me very happy. He calls himself a *fishionary*. I think he may have originated the word. It sure fits him."

Below are just a few others who have followed the dream of using their specific passion as a mission. Because these gentlemen are friends, I include their wives' names along with a few comments from some of them.

Gerry Caillouet: Host of the popular radio show *God's Great Outdoors.*

His wife, Cindi, says,

> Gerry sees his love for hunting as more than just a recreational interest. Not long after his own conversion, he began pursuing a way to use what he loved to do to serve God and to reach other outdoorsmen and women, boys and girls with the gospel of Jesus Christ. He organized a nine-day bow-hunting camp in central Ohio. Out of that incredibly effective outreach came the idea to start a radio program that would reach further than our hollows here

in Ohio. The broadcast has been an immense amount of rewarding work for him. Eventually he decided to write a book called *Hunting Blunders and the One that Got Away,* which has been used to touch a lot of lives. It never ceases to amaze me how God has changed Gerry from someone who once hunted for his own pleasure to someone who now finds great pleasure in "hunting for others" who need the Gospel.

Dr. Jimmy Sites: Host of the widely viewed TV show, *Spiritual Outdoor Adventures.*

Jimmy's wife, Amanda, has stood faithfully beside him through his decision to change from a pulpit pastor to TV hunting guide, leading men and women to a relationship with their Creator through the visual arts.

Jeff Means: Founder and president of the Dallas, TX, based motorcycle ministry called "Fellowship Riders."

Megan, his wife, can often be found seated snug behind Jeff as they travel the open Texas highways on their Harley Davidson. Fellowship Riders has become Jeff's motorcycle mission for the purpose of leading bikers down the highway to heaven. Megan writes,

> When Jeff asked me if he could get a motorcycle, I thought it sounded fun...but dangerous. I had always grown up with a fear of them. After taking the motorcycle safety course and seeing that his excitement was like that of a little boy, how could I not have agreed? But after a couple of years of riding and meeting other guys, there was still something missing. He just didn't know what it was. It was after we started going to a new church that he decided to connect with other riders in that congregation. Finding some solid camaraderie with some of the riders at the

church, he contacted the pastor and asked if he could start a rider's group.

Wow! What a life change. Four years later, 800-plus riders have joined in. Their goal is to spread the word about the joy found in mixing rides and fellowship. Jeff has even baptized some of the riders in lakes or rivers along the roads they have ridden. He has made such an impact on so many lives, and he's been blessed with a host of friends. And with all of that, he still holds down a full-time job and continues to be the best husband to me and the best dad in the whole world to our girls.

Dan Field: Dan, along with his partners, David McGill and Steve Rotramel, formed "Provision Productions" to encourage vital and thriving family relationships through hunting videos. "Outdoor Journey" is an exciting and entertaining visual resource for hunter/dads.

Dan's wife, Sherry, has been his main supporter in the cause. She sent this e-mail:

> What I appreciate most about Danny and his partners and their "Outdoor Journey" video is how strongly they felt led to help other men ensure that the great heritage of hunting be passed on to their children. Not only did they want to offer a "pure" image of hunting (hits *and* misses, too), they also wanted to use their love for the outdoors for another cause. They were driven by the goal of letting others know of the importance of establishing and maintaining a relationship with the Father in heaven through a walk with His Son, Jesus Christ.
>
> Being an avid outdoorsperson myself, I know how inspiring being outside can be. For some wives, however, it is a giant leap to understand this about their men. But much to Danny's delight, after watching the video, some

ladies have even encouraged their husbands to do more hunting, especially with their kids. I am profoundly proud of Danny's willingness to give so much of himself to others.

Brodie Swisher: Executive director of The Covenant Ranch in Paris, TN, dedicated to changing the lives of youth through adventures in the great outdoors. Also, Brodie is a world champion game caller, an outdoor writer, videographer, and seminar speaker.

Brodie's wife, Amanda, candidly reveals,

> I had no idea what I was getting into when I walked down the aisle of that country church to stand by my husband in marriage. I did not realize that on that day I was marrying such an avid outdoorsman. Not growing up in a family that loved to hunt, I had a hard time understanding Brodie's passion for leaving the warmth of our bed in the early morning hours to pursue deer, turkey, and ducks. And the season never ends in our house. He is always practicing his skill of game calling.
>
> While I was not necessarily overjoyed with his hobby at first, a gradual change came as I began to see how Brodie loved to use his interest as a way to encourage and teach people of all ages, especially the young people. I could see that to him his hobby was a tool and not merely a toy. Just as it says in the Bible that God has called some to be teachers, some to be preachers, and so on, I can see that God has put His favor on Brodie and given him the pulpit of the great outdoors. I know heaven will be an exciting time as we encounter the countless numbers of folks, young and old, who have been touched by my husband's work.

I could fill up more pages with examples of men who have managed to do more with their hobbies than just disappear from the house. While most of them have a mission that may not receive media attention, be found on a bookshelf, or seen on TV, the impact on others is just as significant. There are hunters who love to supply pre-dressed and prepackaged venison each year for families with lots of kids. Others have chosen to assist handicapped hunters in their love of the outdoors. One fellow I met enjoys using his ski boat to entertain inner-city youth who attend a summer camp. On and on the opportunities go. While these men are to be congratulated for their service to others, their wives are also to be applauded for the support they have given to their husbands' choices to make the leap from passion to mission.

The obvious question is, In what way might your hobby become more than just a thing for your "self"? Is there something you could do with your passion to help others? While many of us might have a tendency to initially think we have to do something spectacular, the key is to start with a small step. Begin with the thing that is closest to us. In the book of Exodus, chapter 4, God asked Moses, "What is that in your hand?" Moses said, "A staff."

God told His faithful servant to throw the staff on the ground, and it became a snake. Then God told Moses to pick it up and when he did, it turned back into a staff. This was done for the purpose of revealing to all who were standing by and watching that God had appeared to Moses and that his authority could be trusted. The point of this story in the context of turning your passion into a mission is that God didn't have to ask Moses to run out and find something to use to accomplish His purpose. The item was already in Moses' hands. And the same could be true for you as well. The thing you are looking for may already be in the hands of your heart. It's called your hobby. You don't have to go far to find it, and best of all you can start small.

The friends I highlighted in this chapter started with simple things like a roll of film, a few rods and reels, a cassette tape, a video camera, a motorcycle, and a handful of game calls. In my case, I started with writing just one page and then going to the next. For Annie, my small beginning was a huge advantage for her because the change was a manageable adjustment. I just altered the amount of thought time I gave to writing and pecked away from time to time at a computer keyboard. Eventually, the vision for pouring encouraging insights into the hearts of other outdoorsmen through writing began to unfold.

You too can do something with the "staff" that is in your hands. Just move slowly and patiently—and be sure to let your wife know what you are doing. When she sees that your passion is becoming a mission, her level of appreciation of your interest will grow day by day.

9

Attempting
the Impossible

When our son's friend Joey announced that he was getting married, I volunteered to put together a counterpart to the bridal shower that his family was planning for his bride-to-be. It would be called "A Tool Shower."

The guidelines for the male-only party were that everyone would come hungry and fully aware that their wives would have to endure the serious aftereffects of the beans in the venison chili Annie made for the entire group. Also, the men's entry ticket would be two things: First, a duplicate of one of their own tools they used to maintain their houses or apartments, and second, each fellow would be prepared to give Joey one helpful hint about being a good husband or handyman.

The affair was a huge success. Most of the married guys were envious of all the new shiny gadgets Joey received. We were especially drooling over all the glossy plastic cards that could be carried into one of our super hardware centers and exchanged for manly "stuff." The haul of tools and things Joey received was significant, and we assured him that when the moment arrived for him to come to the domestic aid of his young bride, his new collection would ensure him "hero status."

As the evening was about to end, we got to the helpful hints portion of the event. One by one the guys offered the groom-to-be their best tips for both husbandry and household maintenance. Of all that was said, none of the advice matched what Joey's grandfather had for the young groom. When it came his turn, the 80-year-old sighed deeply and leaned way back on the chair where he sat. Then he turned his head slightly as he slid his weathered hand across his mouth. We all waited quietly. Following one more well-timed sigh, Mr. Wilson spoke with a slow, confident, and seasoned voice. "Joey…there's only two things about a woman that a man needs to know…but ain't nobody knows what they are!"

The room came unglued with laughter. We had been set up by a real pro. Problem was, we all knew he was right on target. Poor Joey! All us older guys wondered how he would handle such intense truth. And I've thought often about what Mr. Wilson said to his grandson. I chuckle every time I remember it. In fact, I use his quip from time to time in our concerts. (I borrow from the best!)

As mysterious as woman can be, what I want to do now is attempt the impossible. I'd like to try to take a guess at what those two unknown things are that men don't understand about women but desperately need to know. I am fully aware that there are many more than two, but just for the sake of accepting the challenge that is presented in Mr. Wilson's wit, here goes.

Thing #1 that every man ought to know about women:

We need them!

Because I accept and embrace the biblical account of how human beings came into existence, I also believe in the Creator's assessment of the male version of humanity noted in Genesis 2:18: "It is not good for the man to be alone."

God had said about everything else He had done up to that point, "It is good." The creation of the earth, sun, moon, sky, beasts of the fields, birds of the sky, and fish of the sea were all good to God. The first time He said something was not good was in reference to Adam.

Interestingly enough, at that point Adam was living in a perfect world and in a perfect state of health and spirit. Sickness and sin were not issues. Instead, it was the first man's aloneness

The Good Husband's Principle

Men need women

that motivated God to announce that something was not yet complete. For man to be without a companion was not a good thing to God. And if it's not a good thing to Him, then who are we to disagree? To agree with God is always a smart thing.

The good news is that the fact that Adam, the first man, was in need of a helper did not represent a flaw in his construction. Much to the contrary, it can be said that man's need for woman was ultimately a divine design. For one reason, there was work to be done in tending the garden of Eden, and God knew very well that Adam could use some help.

I am living proof that the need a man has for a woman has not faded since the ancient days of creation. First of all, I could not do what I feel compelled to do as a vocation without Annie's help. Standing solo in front of audiences delivering songs and stories for the purpose of building stronger families is something I do from time to time, but to be quite honest, I feel very incomplete and a bit inadequate when I'm up there by myself. It's a scary thing to do. For that reason, I cherish what Annie brings to the stage. Her insight and intelligence, as well as her incredible depth of understanding human behavior through the eyes of the Scriptures are contributions that I would not care to do without.

Besides my need for Annie's help in our work, there are also practical reasons I need her. For example, I know I would be a total social slob without Annie to help me. I know how to get dressed when I go hunting. Choosing the right camo pattern is not a problem. When the leaves are on the trees and there are shadows in the woods, I wear a darker color camo. When the leaves are off the trees and there's a lot of light, I wear a lighter color camo. That's a no-brainer for me. However, getting myself ready for the rest of the world usually results in a pitiful attempt at best. To avoid being a complete fashion failure, I look to Annie for assistance. It is simply the smart thing to do. She's happy, and I'm usually decent and presentable.

In addition to the need a person has for a teammate to help with the daily work that must be done, the book of Ecclesiastes (4:9-12) lists at least three other ways people need each other. While this passage was originally written about friendships, the truth is very applicable to the relationships between husbands and wives. In the text we learn that as teammates, two people can fend off a thief more effectively than one, if one falls down the other can help him up, and when it's cold, two can lie down and warm one another.

If men will admit it, most would concede that the need for woman is obvious and undeniable. To think we guys can get along without the gals is to believe a lock does not need a key or a rose does not need the morning dew or a river does not need an ocean.

If a fellow's need for a woman is so real and ongoing, doesn't it make you wonder why any husband would refuse to consider his wife's feelings when it comes to whether or not she appreciates what he likes to do? Furthermore, why would any of us refuse to be fair with her when it comes to our resources, time, words, childcare, and the other issues?

Thing #2 that every man ought to know about the woman:

She likes change!

Actually, there's a second part to the statement "*She likes change.*" It is, *And men really don't care for it at all!* It appears that we men may be more like God than women are because we are "the same yesterday, today, and forever!" Most of us could go a long time before we'd even remotely consider altering anything.

For example, some of us have the same hairdo we had in the fifties (that's 1950), if we have hair. Others of us drive a Chevy or a Ford today because we drove one make or the other back when we were teenagers. Furthermore, our philosophy when it comes to things like cars, hair, furniture arrangements, kitchen table placement, pictures on the wall, and the bowl we use for our cereal is: *If it's fixed, don't break it.*

The Good Husband's Principle

Women like change

The disturbing news is that we live with a creature (and I use the word very respectfully) who is constantly changing. One of my favorite stories to tell about how I have come to accept the ever-changing wife that God gave me involves wall paint.

Annie called me into our home's entryway one morning and as we stood there looking at it, she asked, "Don't you think this off-white would look good if it were a pale yellow?"

When she said the words, I heard the cha-ching of the cash register at the paint store as they took our hard-earned money. I felt the stinging pain in the back of my legs that would come from standing precariously on tall ladders for hours. It took only a millisecond for me to start searching my brain for a shield that would repel the work spear that had just been thrown at me.

I looked around the cavernous area we stood in and, with my very best attempt at getting myself out of the pain of hard labor, I responded, "Well, Babe, if it's pale yellow you want...time will do that for us."

Annie managed a charity chuckle at my little bit of humor. I actually thought it was a brilliant line, but we both knew I had failed miserably at warding off the inevitable. Today, the entryway is pale yellow. Its color is visual evidence to me that women love change.

Fellows, if you can grasp and accept the truth that your wife, by her very nature, is likely a huge fan of change, it will greatly assist you in being willing to give a try to my final and most important suggestion regarding her appreciation of your hobby. It is:

Let your interest become an instrument of personal change.

I have seen the beneficial results of using my passion for hunting as an instrument of change. One example that I love to give comes from an experience as a deer hunter that I wrote about in *A Look at Life from a Deer Stand*. The story began on an early morning in West Virginia.

I was sitting in a treestand that my brother-in-law had built for me, and I had yet to see a deer. Suddenly the crashing sound of deer hooves in the dry leaves alerted me that there were deer nearby. A few moments later, a buck came by me running at full speed, chasing a doe. Since it was mating season for the whitetails, I knew I had just witnessed a classic example of what dangerous effects the mating urge can have on a buck's usually cautious behavior.

The older males in the deer world are, by nature, extremely wary. They are generally very hard to outsmart. However, during rut their usually alert attitude is interrupted by a strange abandonment of that cautiousness. They step completely out of their good sense that protects them most of the year, and for about five weeks or so they engage in an uncontrolled pursuit of the "accepting" female deer.

The vulnerability that results makes the buck a primary target for hunters who happen to be in the right place waiting for him. And that's exactly what I was doing. When the buck ran by my stand the first time, I drew a bead with the open sights of my rifle and blasted two shots at him. The fresh craters in the dirt behind him told me that my bullets did not find their intended mark.

I was dealing with some major disappointment as the woods became quiet again. I began to rehearse an explanation for my missed shots that I would have to give to Annie's two brothers who were hunting close by. While I was forming my statement, I heard some ruckus in the leaves to my left. Lo and behold, the same two deer came running by me again. I took a second pair of shots at the buck...and missed again.

The buck never once flinched at the deafening sound of the rifle. He didn't even bother to look my way. He was intently focused on his quest for love. However, I have always wondered if that smart doe knew I was there. Maybe she brought that old buck back by me hoping I would connect. In fact, I thought I heard a voice screaming as they ran by me that second time, "Shoot him! Shoot him!" Maybe not...then again...

The point is, that day held more than just some exciting hunting action for me. It also became a moment when I was changed as a husband because after pondering the scene that had unfolded below me, I came to a conclusion—one that I knew would be meaningful and important to Annie. I described the morning's events to her, and in so many words I said, "Babe, I know the Devil doesn't like me and wants to destroy me. And here's what I learned in the woods today. If I act like a stupid buck and go chasin' women, I'm gonna get shot at. I don't want to do that 'cause fact is, he's not likely gonna miss!"

> **The Good Husband's Principle**
>
> **Let your interest become an instrument for change**

With words that only a deer hunter's wife could understand and appreciate, I had told her that something very important had happened while I was out there and it had changed me "in here" (in my heart).

Annie was obviously grateful that my time in the woods had resulted in a renewed determination to be morally careful. From then on, each time I picked up on a new character-building insight while hunting, I made it a point to reveal it to my wife. Invariably, she would express her joy for how hunting improved my character.

Eventually I decided to put my determination to be a "smart buck" into a lyric. Sometimes it's the best way songwriters can share their feelings. This lyric was intended to give my wife the assurance of my resolve to remain faithful.

What I Wouldn't Give

She gave that signal,
She had that walk.
Something inside me
Began to talk...
Said, "Aint she fine?"
I said, "I agree."
I felt the danger when she looked at me.

I started thinkin'
How she would feel.
I started wonderin'
How I might close the deal.
I could say I didn't,
When I really did.
If I could have her, what I wouldn't give.
Ooh, what I wouldn't give.

My wife...
Her smile,
Our memories.
The miles
Our children
Their trust
And everything that God has given us—
That's what I wouldn't give
For her.

It's not my first time,
And there'll be more.
There's a million battles
In this one war.
But God knows
I want to win,
So what I wouldn't give for her
Let me say it again.

My wife…
Her smile
Our memories.
The miles
Our children
Their trust
And everything that God has given us.
That's what I wouldn't give
For her.[5]

Maybe you have never given any consideration to beginning an active search for ways that your interest could become a source of change in your life. It's not too late. There are life-altering truths that can be harvested from nearly anything that a man enjoys doing. Below are three other things I like to do in the great outdoors besides hunting and how they have garnered something meaningful to Annie.

Fishing. While fishing one day on Old Hickory Lake in our middle-Tennessee area, I managed to land a sizable bass. I was elated. But there was no one around to share the joy. That day I realized that the excitement that comes with catching a big fish doubles when there's someone there to be happy with you. And if the brute happens to shake the hook, the disappointment is only half as bad when there is someone there to share the pain of an empty stringer.

I told Annie later about how I had felt that day, and that it made me treasure our relationship even more. I said, "Having you in my life means that the joys are doubled and the sorrows are halved." She smiled.

Motorcycling/Bicycling. Vehicles with two wheels hold the interest of a lot of guys from boyhood to...well...taller boyhood. It is certainly true for me. And I don't mind doing my own maintenance. Included on the list of things to take care of are wheels. Amazingly, there is a picture of a healthy family on every motorcycle or bicycle wheel just waiting to be discovered. I pointed it out to Annie one day, and she has never looked at either machine the same way since.

Here's the picture: The wheel is the family unit, the spokes are the family members, and the hub is the central focal point for everyone to come to. For our family, the hub is a relationship with God through Jesus Christ. If every family member daily follows the line of their spoke as it moves toward the hub, then everyone in the family is drawing closer together. It is a simple but profoundly important analogy that our entire family has appreciated...and it came from a simple two-wheeled toy.

Golf. One of my personality flaws is that I can get really bent out of shape if I fail to reach the pinnacle of perfection when I do something. At times, if I have given in to this attitude, those around me have suffered through my unhappiness. Thankfully, there was something to be learned in the outdoors that gave me a new meaning to an old problem.

I like the game of golf, and I have actually played in The Masters...The Masters of Mediocrity that is. Really, I've had enough disappointing rounds with friends to have heard one particular statement over and over again. Those two words are: "That'll play." They are not unkind words, nor could they be classified as the compliment that a golfer likes to hear about his shot. "That'll play" is simply a recognition by those who stand by and watch your ball leave the tee box that your shot may not have landed where you intended, but at least it is still somewhere on the planet and maybe even near the fairway. In other words, "We'll see you later on the green...a lot later!"

Because I have had many opportunities to ponder the two words, I finally came upon a comparison between them and two words in the Bible, "Well done." It occurred to me that when we get to heaven, God is not going to say to any of us who have played the course of life, "Best done." All we get for our very best efforts is a "Well done." The truth is, only One has done life best. His name is Jesus Christ.

I informed Annie about the "golf course revelation" and that while I would not stop doing all that I could to at least hear a "well done" in heaven, I would try not to be so uptight when I don't hear "best done" down here on earth. The whole idea has caused me to relax regarding the frailty of my humanness, and it has undoubtedly benefited my wife.

On that note, I leave you with some wisdom I once heard:

> It is better to fail in a cause that will ultimately succeed
> than to succeed in a cause that will ultimately fail.

My fellow hobbyists, may I urge you to not give up in your quest to help your wife not hate what you love to do? You will not do everything absolutely perfectly. You and I both know it. However, if you truly desire it, the goal of gaining her favor is something at which I am sure you will eventually find triumph. Seeking to keep your wife's love and her good will is a great success in itself. Now, may God help you to go and do it right, and may His blessings be on you as you do.

10

Signals

Years ago, when smoking was allowed on airplanes, I was a much more confident flyer. Why? Because of signals! That's right. When a jetliner left the ground and reached a certain altitude prescribed by the FAA, the "no smoking" light would go out on the panel above my head. To me that meant one thing. It did *not* mean that I would remove a pack of cigarettes and proceed to light up. No way. I never believed that it was a good idea to let people create little personal fires in their seats while sitting in a machine that was basically a flying gas station.

Instead, an extinguished "no smoking" lamp indicated that the pilots were satisfied that everything was going A-OK in the cockpit. At least, that's what I believe a veteran flight attendant meant when I overheard him say, "Pilots will not turn out the no smoking light unless they are absolutely certain that all systems are in good working order." He continued, "If that light doesn't go out, that's when you can start to worry!"

After the day I gained that bit of inside information, I thought of those words each time the engines revved up and my flight began that treacherous roll down the runway. I refused to relax until... finally, that telltale spot on the panel was no longer illuminated.

Sadly, something awful eventually happened. As a result, that comforting procedure I needed so desperately was gone. Thanks to some very talented, well-funded, and well-meaning activists, smoking was banned on airplanes. Consequently, the light has never gone out again. Without that signal, I began to deal with anxiety from the moment the wheels went up until they touched down.

I know I was among the vast minority, but I would've almost been willing to go back to the days of suffocation, residual stinkiness on my clothes and hair, and escalating ticket prices due to the high cost of cabin filters just for the sake of the signal. I do believe I could've endured those things again just to know that the pilots were singing a happy song up front.

Then one day, while talking to another flyer about my "disorder," I heard some good news. He said, "The bells...listen for the bells. Dings have replaced the 'no smoking' lamp signal. Most airlines use two bells. Learn their timing. Usually at about 10,000 feet in the ascent, they will ring two dings that almost sound casual or unhurried. This pair of bells lets the attendants know it is okay to unbuckle their seat belts and begin the planned cabin service. That will be your cue that the pilots are satisfied that everything is in good working order."

I was grateful for such useful knowledge, and I would have been happier if he had stopped there. However, he continued with a maniacal grin. "If they don't ring the two bells during the ascent but instead they sound an unusually quick, hurried pattern of four bells, that will be your signal to...well...pray!" I have never forgotten his insight.

There's a picture in the very personal detail about my flight fears that I just revealed. I am a real fan of signals. Especially the ones that tell me something that I desperately need to know. And, as a husband who has a serious hobby, there is a certain signal from Annie that I long for that tells me whether or not all systems are go when I am departing on my flights of fun. In my case, the signal I listen for comes in the form of two words…just like two comforting airplane bells.

The Two Bells

A mere pair of words is all I need from Annie to indicate that things are well between me, her, and my passion for hunting. They are: *"Have fun!"* This little send off says more to this hunter than any other words my wife can say as I leave. This is true because after all these years of flying out of the door during hunting seasons, I finally caught on to the hidden meaning in those two words.

Basically "Have fun!" can be translated,

> I know you've been working hard and you need a break. You've been faithful to make sure our time together has been sufficient. You are fair with our funds, and most important, I trust that you'll be safe 'cause I know that you know I want you to come back to me alive and in one piece. Therefore, I'm confident that you won't do anything intentionally to risk your health. Furthermore, I appreciate the fact that while you're out there you'll be looking for more than just wild critters that can fill our freezer. I know that in the past you've learned so much about life by just being in God's creation. So I look forward to hearing what good things He may show you today through nature. And I know that while you're out there, you'll be praying for me and the kids 'cause you tell me it's a wonderful place to do that. And besides, I can feel your prayers for me and I am grateful. God bless you as you go.

Believe it or not, even though it sounds like a serious case of reading between the bells, that's what I hear when Annie says, "Have fun!" My heart leaps in my chest with rejoicing because I know when she says them I can depart for the woods free of guilt. Oh, my brothers, I long for you to know that joy!

Before I go on, I must tell you about two other words that I often hear when I get back that tells me she's not only pleased but that she is actually interested in my interest. They are: *"See anything?"*

This question is usually accompanied by a slight smile. That little grin is a sign to me that she wants to know whether or not I had a good time. She seems to understand that hunters will often gauge the quality of a hunt not by just a harvest, but also by whether or not they see critters. I suppose she has experienced enough of my empty-handed returns from the woods to know that when I answer the "see anything" question with a sad "Nothing," then in my opinion it didn't go so well. However, she apparently has figured out that I must have had a great time when I respond with an excited, "Yep, saw several. Didn't get close enough to 'em, but they're there!" With that answer she can accurately assume that I had an enjoyable break from the rest of the world.

One other valuable note about "See anything?" that I've learned: Even though the question sounds like she wants to hear the details, most women don't want long, drawn-out descriptions about a hunt, unless they too are hunters. They may not enjoy hearing, for example, a bow-hunting husband tell about the incredibly exciting sound of that first telltale crunch in the leaves that says a deer is coming. They won't understand about the buck-fever-induced sweat in the eyes that made the sight pins hard to see. And they probably will not appreciate the part about the nervous shake that challenges a steady hand, the pass through of the arrow, nor about the blood trail that was almost lost but finally found.

(I don't know about you, but I get excited just writing these descriptions of a bow hunt. Maybe you're a bow-hunter and you felt the excitement too. Calm down, now.)

As thrilling as the challenge can be to hunters, most wives would rather the report not include all those details but instead just a brief overview of the experience. They would probably like the story concise and to the point, perhaps like this: "Very exciting hunt! Saw some really nice deer! Thanks *so* much for the break. I needed it. I love ya, Babe! Can I take you out for dinner?"

A lot of us hunters would love to pour our hearts out to our wives and recount the kill in vivid detail. Some of us long to do so in hopes it would help them understand why we like to do it so much. But according to most of the wives of the friends I hunt with, they would rather we save the fine points for hunting camp or other times we guys gather. I encourage you to not attempt endearing her to the hunt with the fine points of your trip. I know it seems odd, but in most cases you'll do more to help her appreciate it by sparing her from the "paralysis of analysis."

The Danger Bells

While an airline might use four quick bells as a warning that something is wrong, I, as a hunter/husband listen for an alert signal that is double that number. They are:

"What time do you think you'll be back?"

If this question is delivered quick-paced and with a low voice, if each word is somewhat hammered, then very likely something is wrong in the cockpit of Annie's mind. Have I gone hunting too frequently? Have I missed or was I late for one too many appointments (traditions)? Not done my fair share with the kids? Impacted the budget more than a fair share? Failed in the "time together" area? Or not fulfilled safety expectations?

If those ominous eight bells sound, I know it's time to get serious about how I'm handling the balance between her, our relationship, and my hobby. If I refuse to do so, the hard ground of conflict awaits.

Most wives, like mine, will let us know how we are doing as hobbyists if we are attentive to their signals. And as much as I'd like to never "crash," I know that sooner or later it may happen. Thankfully, Annie and I have a mutual understanding in regard to this likelihood that I hope you and your wife enjoy too.

Basically, we don't expect a whole lot out of each other. If she expects perfection out of me, then I can expect the same from her. Thankfully, we agree to not operate that way. We both know that none of us are going to be perfect at all times. While that understanding does not excuse either of us from honestly trying to be our best as spouses, we offer one another room for error.

Annie understands that I will struggle with consistently keeping her pleased with my hobby, but she also knows that I'm not willing to give up trying. My goal is that if my time on earth is finished before hers, I want to hear her say, "Well done, my good and faithful husband." Maybe it won't be said in such biblical terms, but perhaps if I do things right, and if I happen to leave before she does, she will speak of me in the kind way that our former neighbor spoke of her late husband.

Mary Williams lived next door to us when our children were very small. She was a widow, and our kids loved her. They would even take her flowers on occasion...flowers *from her own garden*. (She didn't care for that too much!)

Very often Mary would come over to sit with our kids while Annie and I would go for a walk. We were grateful for her help. At other times, she would just come and visit. One day while we were having coffee and chatting, I asked, "Mary, what do you miss most about not having John around?" She studied for a moment, then answered, "I miss not having someone to 'what if' with."

Though Annie and I had been married only about three years, we could feel the sorrow her answer contained. We asked her to further explain her response. What she told us has remained in our hearts ever since. Almost 30 years of being married to Annie went by before I fully understood what Mary said that day about her aloneness, about John, and what her greatest wish was. I decided that our late widow neighbor's words about her beloved deserved the legacy of a song.

Maybe what Mary said about her precious one will inspire you as a husband to seriously consider what your wife might say about you in the future. While John was probably just doing the things he felt were right and fair as a husband, little did he know that one day in the future it would win him the coveted prize of Mary's sweet words about the quality of his companionship. And I'm sure he didn't know that his good example would someday influence other husbands like you and me. John is proof that "doing it right" has its rewards, both earthly and eternal.

"What If"

Mary said, "There's a lot of things
I've missed about John
In these fifteen years since he's been gone.
Lord knows it's a mighty long list
If I had to choose just one
He used to ask a question
Sometimes I hear it when I'm all alone.

"He'd say...
'What if...we go out to dinner tonight?
What if...we take a walk in the full moonlight?
What if...we go take in a movie, just me and my best
    friend?'
Oh how I wish

I could 'what if'
With John one more time again."

She said, "It's funny how a question
Can hold so many answers
More than I'd ever need.
I never had to wonder,
I never had to ask,
Did he care about me?

"I feel sad for the women
Who've never known a man
Who understood like mine
Love is a diamond
And if you're gonna have it
You gotta spend some time.

"He'd say...
'What if...we go out to dinner tonight?
What if...we take a walk in the full moonlight?
Or what if...we take a ride on the Harley
    just you and me in the wind?'
Oh how I wish
I could 'what if'
With John one more time again.

"He'd say...
'What if...we go out to dinner tonight?
What if...we take a walk in the full moonlight?
Or what if...we go look at antiques?
 Just wanna be with my best friend'
Oh how I wish
I could 'what if'
With John one more time again."[6]

The Questionnaires

The following pages contain the nonscientific questionnaires that were completed by approximately 200 men and women. I include these questions for your enjoyment as well as the helpful insights that your answers (if you choose to fill in the blanks) might reveal. With some of the questions I have included the average outcome from the surveys I sent out, and with others I added the responses that were either typical or that I found very interesting or educational. I hope you glean something useful from this exercise. And maybe you'll even be brave enough to let your wife see the questionnaire designed for the ladies. If you do…you're a brave man—and you'll learn a lot from her responses!

The Men's Questionnaire

Years married _____ (average was 14)

# of children _____ (avg. 2.1—I'd like to meet the .1 kid!)

Age range _____ (infants through 30+)

Occupation _____ (every type from welders to CPAs to airline pilots)

Your favorite outdoor activity or hobby _____

(The list was long but included hunting, fishing, golf, motorcycling, hiking, camping, softball, 4-wheeling, fly fishing, exploring, hockey, sky diving, scuba diving, rappelling/rock climbing, photography, and hang-gliding.)

Frequency of engaging in this activity: Daily __ Weekly __ Monthly__

(Most answered weekly)

Would you consider it dangerous? Yes___ No___ If yes, why?

(Mostly no was answered. Those who most frequently answered yes in order of frequency, were: motorcycling, 4-wheelers, rock climbing, hang-gliding, rappelling, hockey.)

Do you involve your children in your activity? Yes___ No ___

(Most answered yes. Motorcyclists answered no most frequently.)

If you involve your children, is it... Often__ Occasionally ___ Rarely___ (Most: Occasionally)

Number of close friends who join you: ___ Often___
Occasionally___

(The less the number, the more often friends would join in)

Estimated dollar value of all equipment used in this activity:
$_____

(There was an odd mixture. For example, one fellow's bicycle cost $3500 and yet another husband's sailboat was $1000. The amount of money spent was all over the board. The average cost of equipment seemed to be around $750. As you will see on the questionnaire for the ladies that follows, the wives were not asked to estimate dollars spent but to reveal their feelings about their husbands' spending. I wanted to spare the men from trouble in case their wives got hold of their answers!)

What equipment/item are you planning to add or would like to add to your inventory?

(Again, the answers varied. There were items such as motor-cycle windshields, baseball gloves, more rope for climbing, "Big Bertha" golf clubs, guns, bows, arrows, hockey skates.)

Projected cost of these new items? $_____

(It got very interesting here too. The highest figure I saw was $18,000, the cost of a new motorcycle. The lowest was $16 for two boxes of shotgun shells. But my favorite answer was "I'm done." I admire that determination, but I have a feeling this guy was fresh off the purchase of something big. Very often "I'm done" is a promise that a man makes to his "sale-shocked wife" if he detects that she may be overwhelmed by the amount of groceries sacrificed for his new toy.

How would you describe your wife's feelings about what you love to do?

(Here are some answers I received.)

❑ She understands how much it means to me and knows it is my basic form of recreation, something that helps me cope with the stresses of life. (Firefighter/Hunter)

❑ She's okay with it, and loves for me to play with my sons. (CEO/Golfer)

❑ Fearful. (Computer networker/Mountain climber)

❑ It takes time away from her, and I think she's jealous of the time I spend at it. My twin brother is my best buddy, and she is somewhat resentful of that. (Forester/Hunts and fishes)

❑ She tolerates it. She's just glad I don't sit around the house in my underwear and watch ball games. (Engineer/Skeet shooting)

❑ She wants me to go, and she dreams of a full freezer. (Teacher/hunter...and dreamer too!)

❑ She enjoys that I get out. I row and exercise in the morning. I get the kids ready after that. She loves my body, and that's why we have five kids! (Real-estate sales/Rowing/Physical conditioning)

❑ Indifferent. (Appraiser/Hockey)

❑ Supportive as long as I keep the priorities in the right order—God, family, work, then hobby. (Minnow farmer/ Fishing)

❑ Tolerant, sometimes even accepting. (Manager/Anything automotive)

Does she participate in your favorite hobby? _____ If yes, is it... Often__ Occasionally__ Rarely__

(Most answered "Rarely.")

The following is a trio of related questions. Responses to all three are included after them:

A) If there is a problem area, great or small, related to your interest as it pertains to your marriage, can you identify it?

B) If you could say something briefly to your wife about this conflict, what would it be?

C) What steps do you plan to take to resolve this conflict?

The responses to the above questions (A, B, and C) are divided by a slash.

❑ Space used. / I'll try to do better at not exploiting my interest if you will be more accepting of it. / I need to try to understand the emotional side instead of just the logical side. (Manager / Automotive sports)

❑ I allow my friends to use my boat unsupervised more than she would like. / It was like that before you came along. You married me this way. Why would you want to change me? / I allow them to use it less than they were before. (Railroad supervisor/ Boating)

❑ I would like to play golf more than I do. / I need you to encourage me to play golf more that I do. / Let's talk about it. (School teacher /Golfer)

❑ Tired when I get in. / I just need time to rest 'cause I love to fish and don't get to do it that much. / Try not to fish too long. (Air conditioning business/Fishing)

❑ No problem. This is my only vice, and she's happy for me. / blank / blank / (Poultry farmer/Duck hunting)

❑ She is very concerned about safety since she was not brought up in a home with guns or bows. / The safety of our sons is of great importance to me. I love them dearly, and this is a great way to teach them responsibility. / I have assured her by taking the kids through the hunter's safety course and making sure we get out of the woods and home when promised.

❑ I don't always return from riding when expected. / I would like to have the freedom to take more extended rides. / I need to talk to her about it. (Retired/Bicycling)

❑ I can hardly feel comfortable just leaving for an hour. / You need to get over it. I need to stay healthy. / (blank) (Physician's Assistant/Running)

❑ Takes time away from family. / I don't consider it a conflict, but I would be more than willing to change any of my plans if it ever became an issue. I do it for the enjoyment, not for the time away. / Nothing (Engineer/Golf)

❑ She doesn't go to the boat races with me. / Please come and go with me. / Nothing's working at this time. (Sales/Speed boats)

❑ No conflict!

❑ Maybe…sometimes…a little too much. / Please leave me alone…not really. / Buy her a lawn mower of her own. (Power company/Yard and garden)

❑ She feels like she is not my number one priority at times. / I love you, and I need this time sometimes to relax and download. / Make sure I prioritize. I need to balance my time vs. her time. (Pastor/Golfer)

How do you personally benefit from your hobby/interest?

(The five most common answers were: relaxes me, I need the physical activity, the diversion helps me cope, time with kids, and friendships are strengthened.

What advice would you give to another husband to help him help his wife appreciate his hobby? (What one thing has worked for you?)

❑ Make sure she is treated as your top priority, and be sure to tell her why your hobby is so important to you. Communicate your expectations about when and how often you'd like to enjoy doing your hobby.

❑ Pray for God to give you wisdom to know what to do and the strength and courage to do it and help her at all times possible with whatever she needs.

❏ Sit down with a calendar and pre-plan an agreed upon time you will spend doing your thing, and then determine to stick to it.

❏ Limit your passions. In other words, pick out one, maybe two things, that you like to do instead of trying to do everything.

❏ Set a time frame around how much of your schedule is consumed by your hobby.

❏ She needs to see an end in sight. For example, deer season runs from September through December where I live. Turkey season goes from late March through the first of May. It helps her to know that what I love to do has its limitations of time. Also, it has helped to set limits within the frame. In other words, not to go out every day of every season.

❏ Include her if she wants to go, be ready to talk to her while you're out there with her, and do the little things for her and with her that you know make her happy.

❏ Try to accept how different she is, and the fact that her needs can be much greater. If you don't believe it, just look at her purse and then look at your wallet. The difference in the size of the two says it all.

❏ Make sure you say "thank you" to her each time you come home from doing what you love to do. It's amazing how different she can seem when she feels appreciated.

❏ Honor her on one of the two weekend days by doing all the cooking and cleaning. I do this on Sundays.

❏ If you are a deer hunter, be careful to tend to personal hygiene. Don't make her smell the pungent "cover scents" that you use. The essence of doe pee is probably not her idea of a sweet aroma. Also, when you go out in public with her, avoid dressing in hunting clothing unless she likes being seen with a man wearing camo. The safest thing to do is to let her help pick out what you'll wear. One more thing, don't ever scold a woman for mistakenly washing your camo in regular detergent. That's a load you should do yourself using scent-free soap. I can personally tell you that the night can be long and cold if you ever make her mad about washing your clothes.

❑ Never think of your hobby as a right, only a privilege.

❑ I cannot give advice. I'm failing miserably.

❑ I like to golf and hunt. I've learned that in both I'm going to miss some shots. I've also learned never to whine around my wife about it when it does happen. She doesn't need to be a victim of my disappointment.

❑ If you're a newlywed, involve her right away in your hobby and be sure to show a genuine interest in what she likes to do as well.

❑ The key to success in this area is to put her happiness first. Everyone in my circle of friends agrees that "if mama ain't happy…ain't nobody happy!" We like happy mamas.

❑ Show deference to the reservations she might feel about what you do. Besides my wife and children, I have never enjoyed anything more than hang-gliding. While my wife endures my uncommon hobby, I try to do all I can to calm her fears for my safety.

❑ Sometimes, as it was in my case, it is better to buy a "toy" that is new and not in need of restoring. By trying to save money on a sailboat, I ended up spending all the extra time

I had on the "fixer upper." While I admit that I enjoyed the restoration process, the emotional cost on our marriage was not worth the monetary savings.

❑ If I, as a man, require and buy the best equipment and the latest thing, I should also make sure that my wife, as a woman, at least has a real nice vacuum cleaner. One's wife should be encouraged to have nice stuff too.

I have to comment on this last anonymous response. I absolutely, totally admire this fellow's intentions but I have one suggestion for him and all husbands everywhere. Any time a man gets his wife a gift that benefits the entire household, such as a vacuum cleaner, it usually does not qualify as the "peace offering" needed to help her feel like the funds are spent fairly. Unless her hobby is vacuuming the house (not likely), I would suggest getting her something that contributes to her *personal interest*. A few ideas: tools for her flower garden, oil or acrylic paints and high quality paint brushes, equestrian items if she loves horses, or even furniture *if* (and only if) she loves interior design. Simply put, always avoid items that are used by or benefit both of you or everyone in the family.

The key to getting her the appropriate gift is to ask yourself, "What message is this item going to send to my wife?" A household maintenance device such as a vacuum cleaner might say, "Hey woman, get to work!" or "I want to keep you 'cause you're a mighty fine mule." A woman may need and totally appreciate a new washing machine, but it's not necessarily going to say to her, "You are the most unique and creative woman in the history of womankind." Instead, the message might be, "I want to make it easier for you to keep my skivvies clean." Things like vacuums and laundry room items are not likely going to reach to the level needed to send her the message that her *personal* hobby is important to you.

While I'm on the subject of giving gifts to wives, I must offer this warning about one specific type of personal gift that can offend her and really create trouble for you. While some ladies love to exercise and even consider it their personal "outlet," most women (at least the ones I know) are not doing it because they enjoy it. The majority of ladies exercise because they feel less than confident about their personal appearance. Their focus is often weight loss or weight control.

The mistake some guys make without even realizing it until it's too late is this: *Without asking them if they want it*, they will go out and buy their wives an exercise machine, such as a treadmill. They bring it home with a smile, set it up, uncover it for the surprise effect, and then wonder why their wives cry at the sight of it. Men are often not aware that an unsolicited exercise machine might tell a woman, "You're blimpin' up, Babe. Time to put some miles under that fat derriere of yours!"

The best thing when getting a gift for a wife is not to try to surprise her. Instead, ask her the one question my wife likes the very most: "What do you want?" Annie wrote an entire book by that title.

I have learned from her that asking a woman what she wants is very refreshing and exciting. Annie also says that while she dearly loves to hear that question around events like her birthday, anniversary, or at Christmastime, hearing it away from those days makes it even more special.

I sincerely hope this questionnaire has provided some helpful insight. And if you decide to fill in the blanks, I encourage you to discuss the questions with your wife and get her reactions. It could actually be an enjoyable, educational exchange.

Now…if you want to know what your wife might be thinking, turn the page and then give your wife the pencil!

The Ladies' Questionnaire

Years married _____ (Because most questionnaires were completed by both husbands and wives, the average years married were the same...14 years)

# of children ____ (Again, 2.1 kids)

Age range of children _____ (same as the men: infants–30+)

What is your husband's favorite hobby/interest?

_____

While there was plenty of variety, from sailing to collecting Indian artifacts, many of the answers were worded differently than the men. Nearly 100 percent of the guys responded with just one word to describe their hobbies such as *hunting, fishing, golf, hockey*. Many of the ladies, on the other hand, wrote responses that were more lengthy and insightful. Their answers contained observations such as "He watches sports a lot" or "He goes deer hunting often" or "He's a workaholic; all he does is work!" I found this to be curious, but in reality it is easy to explain. In essence, the ladies who responded in this way are describing how their husband's hobby is ultimately affecting *him* and *them*. There is emotion in their responses.

How often does he engage in his interest? Daily__ # of times Weekly ___ Monthly ___

The average for the men was once per week; the ladies observed that their husbands engaged in their hobbies on an average of 2 to 3 times per week. This discrepancy possibly represents how often the men feel like they get to do what they enjoy, and, for the ladies, their contradicting answer may reveal how often they feel abandoned. There's no telling which answers represent the truth.

Do you consider the amount of time he spends on his hobby as... Reasonable____ Somewhat excessive ____ Far too excessive ____

Most ladies answered somewhat excessive.

Do you consider his interest as dangerous? _____ If so, why?

Over 80 percent answered no. Among those who answered yes, most were wives of men who loved to do things that involved motors and weapons such as dirt bikes, motorcycling, flying, guns, and even archery. The most interesting answer was, "Yes, it's dangerous because it limits our time and family life." She felt the danger was more emotional than physical. I don't think most men would have even seen this on their radar. Another woman said, "If he gets seriously hurt or killed, it would leave our family without important support." Obviously, many of the ladies considered the security of herself and her family as the things most threatened by the danger of her husband's favorite sport.

Does he check in with you while he is away from home doing "his thing"? Often ____ Occasionally _____ Rarely ____ Never ____

Most answered occasionally.

Does he involve your children in his hobby? Often ____ Occasionally ____ Rarely ____

Most answered occasionally. Of those who answered often, most of the husbands were fans of water sports. They have boats and/or jet skis—items that seem to be family friendly. Most wives of hunters observed that their husbands rarely took the kids with them.

In what way does his involving the kids personally benefit you and/or your relationship with him?

Most ladies said something like, "It helps the kids feel like he's a part of their lives, and it gives me some much-needed time alone." Sadly, one wife wrote, "He never takes the kids with him. He's happier when he has his 'guy' time." I hurt for this lady, and their children.

Do you participate in his hobby? Often___ Occasionally ___ Rarely___ Never____

Most answered occasionally. However, among those who answered never, most were wives of hunters.

Do you consider his monetary expenditures for things used to support his hobby/interest as reasonable? Yes ___ No___ If not, why?

Amazingly, most wives answered yes. An educational comment was:

❑ "He uses a Cabella's credit card so with his points earned he can get free hunting supplies." (The epitome of industriousness!)

A statement that most men would like to hear was:

❑ "Anything worth doing is worth doing right. I want him to get better equipment but he is too frugal to do it." (Now there's one content lady and a very smart man!)

A sobering comment about the economics of hobbies that showed up more than once was:

❑ "It takes more time than money to do what he enjoys." (Obviously, to these wives' time is more valuable than money.)

If you could say one thing to him about money spent for his hobby/interest, what would you say?

"Fairness" was the most common issue with the ladies. A few of their comments were:

❑ "Let there be a credit card for me and the kids' fun too!" (This request would make any man's legs tremble.)

❑ "Is it really necessary?" (I've heard this one worded slightly different: "Did you really need those arrows?")

❑ "I have a hobby too." (I think I just heard a verbal bullet being chambered!)

While an attitude of fairness (or the lack of it) was addressed, I found it amazing and encouraging that many of the wives had very nice things to say to their husbands about money spent on hobbies. Here's a sampling:

❑ "You deserve the purchases." (He fishes)

❏ "Most of the time I am with you, so at least we're together. It's worth the money!" (This man and his wife love going to professional football games)

❏ "You are the most generous man I know. I don't resent one dime you spend on your hobby. You deserve it." (Thems kissin' words!)

❏ "I appreciate how you try to watch what you spend. It assures me that you will not do anything rash with our family funds." (Pucker up again, Baby!)

If your husband's hobby/interest is seasonal (ex. hunting, fishing), do you feel abandoned during these times?
Yes ___ No ___ If you answered *yes* is it…divided attention ___ lack of help with the children ___ household upkeep ___ conversation ___ other _____

I should have added one more in the options of answers because after this question a large percentage wrote in the word *sometimes* instead of answering yes or no. That indicates that for the most part, guys are doing a fairly good job of balancing their roles as husband and hobbyist. Of course, this is "the glass is half full" view. The ladies might point out the "half empty" side of the matter.

Of those who answered a firm yes, I hate to admit it but nearly 100 percent were wives of hunters. It seems that a lot of us who love the woods have some improvements to make.

Furthermore, of those who answered yes, the feelings of abandonment were in the following areas and are shown in order from most to least: divided attention, conversation, childcare, household upkeep.

If there is one good thing that you see he gleans from his involvement in his hobby/interest, what would it be?

The words, *fulfilled, relaxes,* and *relief* came up a lot in the wife's answers to this question. It was usually worded very much like these responses:

❏ "He seems to be feel fulfilled when he participates in his hobby." (He golfs)

❏ "Hunting relaxes him, and he often comes home in a better mood."

❏ "The stress relief is important to him. I'm glad he gets to do it." (He bicycles)

❏ "His quiet time and communion with God while he is on the water is a source of relaxation and fulfillment for him." (He's an avid fisherman)

❏ "The exercise he gets when he runs keeps him looking very good physically."

❏ "His buddies are good for his emotional and spiritual health. Thankfully, they are really good guys, and I'm glad he gets to be with them." (A hunter with some quality friends. This can be a great blessing to a wife!)

❏ "My husband rides a motorcycle. Even though it makes me a little nervous, I have to tell you that he does what he calls 'prayer rides.' These are rides that he takes around our local schools, elderly folks' homes, and relative's homes. As he does, he prays for those inside. I can't tell you how impressed I am that he would choose to use his hobby for such a redeemable purpose." (Wow! This biker has definitely won the heart of his honey.)

❏ "He is a hunter but loves to read too. I love to see him take books to his stand. His knowledge base has made the quality of our communication even stronger. He's fun to talk to, and reading has done so much for him. I especially am excited when I know he is reading the Bible while deer hunting." (Smart man!)

If there is one thing negative that you see as a result of his hobby/interest, what would it be?

The most common response was not a surprise. It was:

❏ "It takes time away from home and family."

Some comments had practical implications, such as,

❏ "The noise the garage door makes in the early morning when he leaves to go row on the river. It wakes up the kids and me, and I have a hard time going back to sleep."

❏ "When he goes hunting before sunrise, it leaves me with the task of taking all the kids to school."

❏ "As wonderful as riding our horses is, I wonder sometimes if all the money and time spent is worth the fun. Plus, we're getting older now, and the energy required to take care of our animals is more and more draining."

❏ "His love of playing tennis keeps him fit and trim, but the slimmer he looks the frumpier I appear."

❑ "My husband loves shooting trap and skeet. The problem has become his hearing. I have found that I'm having to speak up these days."

❑ "Deer season falls on holidays like Thanksgiving and Christmas." (This issue was covered in the chapter, "Don't Mess with Traditions." This wife's comment serves to highlight a very real potential for conflict between wives, husbands, and their hobbies.)

Some answers had emotional implications, such as:

❑ "It causes feelings of coldness and disconnectedness each year." (Wife of an avid deer hunter who probably becomes far too focused on the wrong trophy during the season.)

❑ "Pride! Killing innocent animals that were minding their own business breaks my heart. But worse, he gets puffed up about it. I don't understand. I learned a great deal about unconditional love through animals, and those lessons have helped me through some of the most difficult times in my life." (I have a feeling this deer hunter's wife has shared her thoughts with him in the past. I can only wonder if he considers how she feels. Also, I can only assume that somehow she didn't know he was a hunter prior to their marriage or maybe he found an interest in it after they married. Either way, there's work to be done in this couple's relationship.)

❑ "He's very protective of his 'stuff' and sometimes yells at me." (Wife of a water skier and avid boater. Obviously, his "stuff" is not the problem. His is a "heart" problem caused by the disease of "self." The moment he begins to act unselfishly toward his wife, that's when there'll be help for him, healing for her, and hope for them.)

What advice would you offer to wives who are married to a man with a serious hobby/interest and who struggle to appreciate that activity?

❑ "If he has been a good husband and father, be sure to encourage him to take some time to enjoy what he likes to do." (Wife of an avid fisherman)

❑ "Someone once said, 'If you as husband and wife work together, it's really OK to have separate hobbies. If you work separate jobs, it might be worthwhile to try to find something you can do together.' They suggested that giving each other's hobbies a try was a place to start. Because we work away from each other every day of the week, we occasionally participate in each other's hobbies on our time off. This has been a wonderful thing to do for us." (He loves sailing, and she enjoys antique restoration)

❑ "If it keeps him from hanging out in bars and chasing women, consider his hobby as a blessing." (This woman's husband loves the game of tennis)

❑ "Take full advantage of each time he offers to help you around the house or with the kids. It will help you and also help him feel better about the time he spends enjoying his hobby." (Her husband plays golf regularly)

❑ "If he invites you to go along, when you can, do it, even if it's only one time. It'll let him know that at least you are interested." (He rides a motorcycle)

❑ "Nagging never helps. It might just drive him deeper into the woods." (Hunter's wife)

❑ "Be sure to develop your own personal interest. Don't just sit around and whine about his." (Wife of a fly fisherman)

❑ "Give him time alone, and do lots of praying!" (He sky-dives!)

❑ "Enjoy the bragging that he does to his friends that you participate with him in his hobby. His joy in being the envy of nearly every husband he knows is my joy too!" (Wife of a motorcyclist)

❑ "Scolding him is bad enough, but doing it in front of your kids is a real no-no. If you have a complaint about what he does or how much he does it, be discreet about when and how loud you converse about the matter." (Wife of a sailboat owner)

❑ "Encourage him to plan ahead. Helping him to see your need for advance notice about what days he wants to enjoy his hobby is important for the functioning of the family schedule." (Hunter's wife)

❑ "Ask him questions about his hobby. Try to find out why he likes it." (Golfer's wife)

❑ "Trade off with him in terms of time spent away from home, especially if you have kids. More than likely, he'll be very willing to give you time to get away in order to spend some on his own. He will love the guilt-free break."

And, gentlemen, with that very last statement, I rest my case.

Notes

1. "The First Winds of Autumn," Steve Chapman-Nannie Walker/Times & Seasons Music, Inc/BMI/2003.

2. "Will You Talk to Me?" Steve Chapman/Times & Seasons Music/BMI/2004.

3. "The Hunter and His Gun," Steve Chapman/Times & Seasons Music, Inc/BMI/April, 2004. Written about Merle Hawn and his three sons in Petersburg, PA.

4. "The Master's Plan," Steve Chapman/Times & Seasons Music, Inc. BMI/2004.

5. "What I Wouldn't Give," Steve Chapman/Times & Seasons Music/BMI/2003.

6. "What If," Steve Chapman/Times & Seasons Music/BMI/2004.

Books, CDs, and Products from the Chapmans

Books

A Look at Life from a Deer Stand
HARVEST HOUSE PUBLISHERS

A Look at Life from a Deer Stand
Gift Edition
HARVEST HOUSE PUBLISHERS

A Hunter's Call
HARVEST HOUSE PUBLISHERS

Full Draw (also known as *The Hunter*)
S&A FAMILY, INC.

Outdoor Insights
S&A FAMILY, INC.

Quiet Moments for Your Soul
HARVEST HOUSE PUBLISHERS

A Hunter Sets His Sights
HARVEST HOUSE PUBLISHERS

Reel Time with God
HARVEST HOUSE PUBLISHERS

With God on a Deer Hunt
HARVEST HOUSE PUBLISHERS

With God on the Open Road
HARVEST HOUSE PUBLISHERS

What Do I Want?
ANNIE CHAPMAN, S&A FAMILY, INC.

*What Husbands and Wives
Aren't Telling Each Other*
STEVE AND ANNIE CHAPMAN,
HARVEST HOUSE PUBLISHERS

10 Things I Want My Son to Know
STEVE CHAPMAN, HARVEST HOUSE PUBLISHERS

10 Things I Want My Daughter to Know
ANNIE CHAPMAN, HARVEST HOUSE PUBLISHERS

Songs

The Master's Plan
TIMES & SEASONS MUSIC, INC/BMI/2004
(NOT YET RECORDED)

First Winds of Autumn
TIMES & SEASONS MUSIC, INC/BMI/2003

Talk to Me
TIMES & SEASONS MUSIC, INC/BMI/2004
(NOT YET RECORDED)

What If
TIMES & SEASONS MUSIC, INC/BMI/2004

The Hunter and His Gun
TIMES & SEASONS MUSIC, INC/BMI/2004
(NOT YET RECORDED)

CDs

Steppin' in the Tracks
S&A FAMILY, INC/2003

Video (DVD & VHS)

Huntin' & Pickin'
S&A Family, Inc/2003

For information about the availability and purchasing of these products or for speaking, singing, or seminar information please contact:

Steve Chapman
S&A Family, Inc
PO Box 535
Madison, TN 37116
or
visit our website:

www.steveandanniechapman.com

Other Good
Harvest House Reading

Becoming What God Intended
David Eckman

Every person's heart life is filled with pictures of reality—often false ones. But as believers use the truth of their new identity in Christ to develop biblical pictures, they will be freed from negative emotions and habitual sins…and finally experience a life that matches what Scripture promises. Dr. Eckman helps you understand your past, balance your emotions, and break free to a new way of living.

Every Marriage Is a Fixer-Upper
Bill and Pam Farrel

The Farrels provide a tool chest of communication skills for do-it-yourselfers who want to get the most out of their marriage. You'll discover how to strengthen the foundation of your family, inspect your marriage for hidden weak spots, and protect your relational investment with consistent maintenance. Packed with practical, biblical insights and real-life solutions.

A Husband After God's Own Heart
Jim George

Highlighting 12 areas that really matter in a marriage, Jim George reveals how your marriage can grow richer and deeper. You'll discover how to win your wife's heart through loving leadership, enjoy better communication through careful listening, build a happier home through wise guidance, encourage you family's spiritual growth by example, and excel at a career without sacrificing family priorities.

Less Is More Leadership
H. Dale Burke

Every leader knows the feeling. You think that if you just work harder, faster, and longer, you'll eventually get on top of the pile. But no matter how hard you try, you feel like the hamster who runs fast and furious only to get off the wheel and find his scenery hasn't changed a bit. *Less Is More Leadership* will transform your leadership and your life, helping you to master the Power of Convictions, the Power of Servant-leadership, the Power of Vision, the Power of Letting Go, and much more.

Romancing Your Wife
Debra White Smith and Daniel W. Smith

You can make your marriage dynamite! Did you know that helping with housework is as appreciated as flowers? "Little gestures" help create a loving atmosphere? And talking and sharing are crucial to a lively relationship? With Debra and Daniel's insights, your marriage can be more dynamic, more passionate, and more intimate than you ever thought possible!

When Good Kids Make Bad Choices
Elyse Fitzpatrick and Jim Newheiser with Dr. Laura Hendrickson

What can you do when your child has gone astray? Speaking from personal experience as parents and as biblical counselors, Jim and Elyse help you deal with your emotions and suggest positive steps you can take in negative situations. Laura provides insightful questions to ask pediatricians and advice regarding medicine prescribed to children.